The Political Spectrum Freedom vs. Enslavement

Second Edition

By David R Young

Volume One of the Freedom vs Enslavement Series

ISBN: 978-0-9858707-3-7

Published by DRY Productions

Cover design by D.R. Young

Second Edition

Printed in the United States of America

For information or bulk orders, contact:
DRYoung.Freedom@gmail.com

Art Credits:

Cover Art: D.R. Young

Graphics: D. R. Young

Portrait: Chanda Brae Photography,
Chandabraephotography.com

TABLE OF CONTENTS

Preface

What is a spectrum?

The rainbow is easily the most recognizable and popular visual representation of the color spectrum. Natural law dictates that the color pattern is always the same.

The gray scale is likely the simplest example of a spectrum.

Black White

Between the extremes of black and white is the spectrum, which fades from a glaring white to the deepest black.

Many spectra are invisible to the eye or senses like the spectrum of radio waves.

Usually, only a small portion of a complete spectrum is useful in day-to-day activities. A thermometer, used for taking body temperature measures a small portion of the broader heat-cold spectrum.

The question I first asked was: “Where does a society, based on the protection of individual rights and freedom, fit on the Political Spectrum?”

If the two ends of the political spectrum are communism and fascism, where does freedom fit in relation to these two extremes?

Just as a body thermometer measures only a small scale of the heat-cold spectrum, I discovered the current political spectrum included only a portion of the entire political spectrum.

I didn't create this political spectrum outlined in this book. Just like a rainbow, it only became fully visible under exact conditions. But once it became visible, it was something to behold.

But the political spectrum had become so confusing, few people even bothered to look for it.

It is impossible to discover something and not want to show it to another. Not to merely share it, but to find out if they could also see it.

Thus, the original book was written. And the response was positive. Others could see it.

One acknowledgment of this book came with a first-place gold award from a writer's contest. One of the award judges had this to say:

"Before you step into any conversation about politics on a national or global level, you must first know the facts. David R. Young's The Political Spectrum: Freedom vs. Enslavement is a unique book that delivers the information one

needs to understand the left, the right and every party in between."

Reader reviews also acknowledged the greater clarity they gained when viewing politics through the prism of this information.

Their comments helped guide the expansion of this 2nd Edition. I appreciate the support and acknowledgement I received from the readers.

Where are we going? This book will take you on a journey of discovery, step by step.

When you reach the final pages, you may find that the real journey is just beginning. Viewing the political landscape of our country will appear much different.

You cannot watch a 3D movie without special glasses to bring it into focus. Likewise, politics cannot be clearly viewed without understanding the full political spectrum.

It will take you far less time to read this book than it took to research, discover and formulate this data. But as your guide, I am very glad and honored to have you along.

Enjoy the adventure!

David R Young

"A wise and frugal Government, which shall restrain men from injuring one another, which shall leave them otherwise free to regulate their own pursuits of industry and improvement, and shall not take from the mouth of labor the bread it has earned. This is the sum of good government..."

Thomas Jefferson

Definition: **Natural Law** - (Noun) a law or body of laws that derives from nature and is believed to be binding upon human actions apart from or in conjunction with laws established by human authority.

Definition: **Politics** - (Noun) the methods or tactics involved in managing a state or government.

Definition: **Spectrum** - (Noun) used to classify something in terms of its position on a scale between two extreme points: *The left or the right of the political spectrum.*

Chapter One

Questions about Government

Teen, ***"It's a free country! I can do whatever I want!"***

Father, ***"As long as you're in my house and I'm paying the bills, you'll do what I say!"***

This typical and often-heard argument is one which captures a portion of the political spectrum.

Ah, the irresponsible freedom of youth - and yet, without that urge, without that sassy spirit, we may have ended up with a completely different form of government than was laid down by the founding fathers.

The second half of the conversation is also very telling. How much of your freedom are you willing to give up for security, both economic and personal safety? It is an important question.

How does a free and prosperous society deteriorate and disappear, only to become a shadow of its former glory? Is the decay caused by internal self-destruction or are there forces exterior to a culture acting to bring it down? Or is it a combination of both?

A nation can self-destruct through several means.

For example, if a culture's education does not include the history and fundamental principles of its founding, then it is inevitable that society will deteriorate or wander from those principles.

Were the Bill of Rights and the U.S. Constitution a part of your or your children's education in school? Most likely not. It is not enough to know that they exist. If you and your children do not read and understand these documents, can you say if they are still in use or being followed? And how would you know if they were being violated?

Self-destruction of a society also occurs when individual responsibility and personal ethics deteriorate. A society is made up of individuals. If the individual deteriorates, so follows society. Increasing illiteracy, drug addiction, and criminality are signs of internal decay.

What of external sources?

A natural law of physics states that a body in motion stays in motion unless acted upon by another force. Could this natural law apply to the formation, longevity and decay of cultures and political systems? If so, what external forces might exist which could bring a whole culture to ruin?

One culture can clash with another, as did the European and Native American societies. An obvious instance of an external force displacing an existing culture.

But what of a strong nation whose moral, technological and military strength prevents any direct confrontation by its enemies?

How might an enemy corrupt its government, erode the morals of its individuals and bring about the demise of that country?

And what must its citizens be educated on to thwart such destructive influences?

What are the political Left and Right?

It seemed a simple question, yet every reference examined either resulted in more questions or greater confusion.

Countless attempts to understand this subject can be found on the internet. Chart after chart has been drawn by people to sort out how the various political systems fit with each other. They all recognized and attempted to address the deficiencies of the current representation of the political spectrum.

During the author's search it appeared no one had a clear-cut answer. In fact, during the research it was found that the subject is so often presented in such a complex and confusing manner, it had to be assumed that either no one understood the spectrum, or it had been made complex and confusing intentionally.

Below are three examples of the political spectrum which can be found online. Notice the similar points. But also notice the differences.

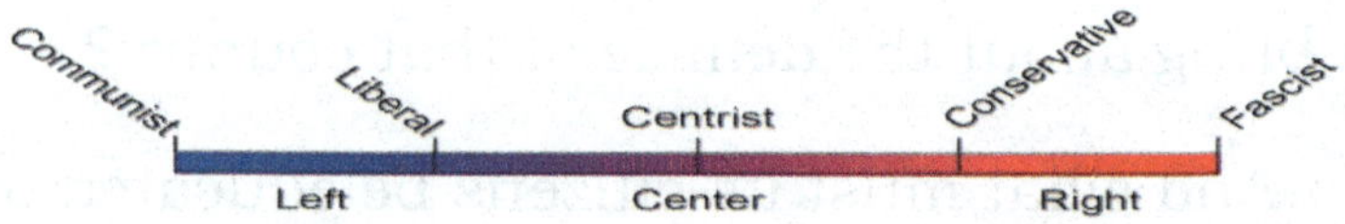

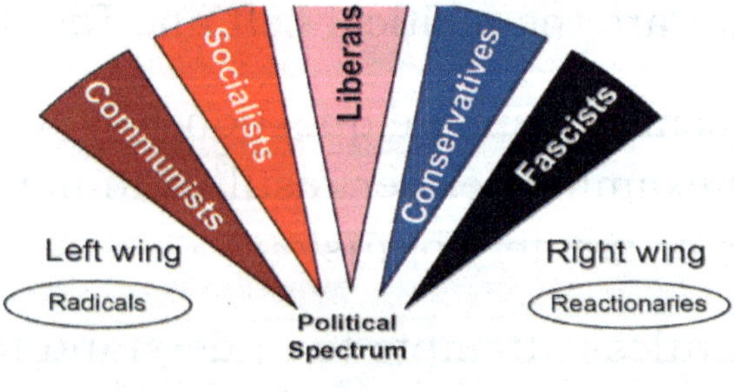

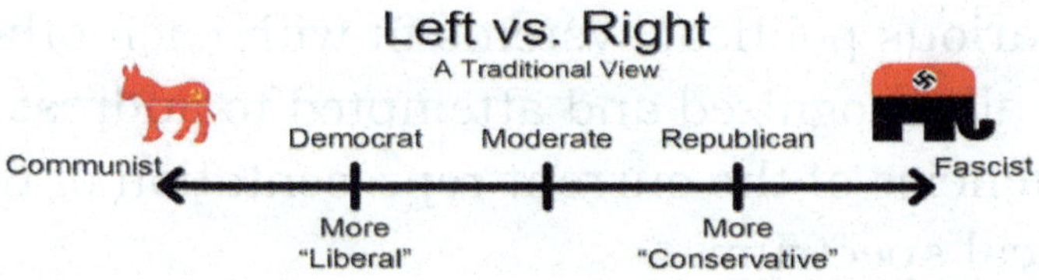

These typical charts neither agree, nor are they accurate. Only two points of the spectrum are held in common in most charts: Communism on the far left and Fascism on the far right. These are the two points most charts seem to agree on. Yet, the use of these two oppressive political systems as a dichotomy is the very reason for the never-ending confusion.

After you have read this book, you will see the political spectrum is very straightforward and easy to work with. It becomes a useful tool, not unlike a pair of glasses which brings things in focus.

The information in this book provides a comprehensive explanation of the various political systems of government. It also shows their relationship with each other, and their relationship to the governed; you.

This book also offers solutions to maintaining, preventing, or reverting the decline or loss of individual rights and freedoms. But it does something even more.

Once understood, it provides a path to continued improvement toward a truly free society, which really hasn't existed before.

If one wants a free society, understanding this information would be necessary to establish workable solutions toward that goal.

Chapter Two

Looking for a workable Dichotomy

The word **Dichotomy**, as it is used in this book, is defined as an absolute contrast or difference of two extremes or opposites. Here are some known dichotomies:

The changing colors or shades between them represent the actual **spectrum**. Any point within a spectrum can be selected, examined, and identified.

The traditional political spectrum begged the question: "Why were Communism and Fascism chosen as the dichotomies of the spectrum, and are they really the extreme ends of the political spectrum?"

They are both oppressive systems of government, so are they a dichotomy?

The two systems are in fact opposed to each other, but they have enforcement of beliefs in common. They also have the individual existing only to serve the group.

Benito Mussolini became the leader of the Fascist Party in Italy in the 1920s.

According to his writings, Fascism is the establishment of *The State* as being above everything and everyone; this meant that all citizens served *The State* and *The State* controlled all.

This authoritarian system allowed private property and privately-owned businesses, but certain freedoms were limited.

For instance, freedom of speech was granted to those who agreed with the concepts of fascism but not to political opposition, such as communism or democracy.

Freedom of the Press disappears as media becomes state-controlled or heavily censored.

Freedom of movement is restricted through internal passports, travel bans, and surveillance.

On the other hand, communism has no love or tolerance for the Fascist State. It is everything the communist despises. One of its stated objectives is to eliminate "*The State*". A world with no countries or borders is envisioned. It also holds as its fundamental concept that private property is the root of all social evil. It attempts to bring about equality for everyone by eliminating all ownership.

Oddly enough, communism attempts to achieve this through an "entity" so fondly and reverently referred to as "*The People*". Under a communist government everything is said to belong to *The People.*

But in practice, as can be seen throughout history and in today's communist countries, everything belongs to the leaders of the communist party.

Individuals are forced to conform with its doctrines or are imprisoned or eliminated — if they haven't already escaped to another country.

Based on the above brief descriptions, one can see the current political dichotomy is based on two oppressive political concepts, *The State* and *The People.*

Dichotomy of Traditional Political Spectrum

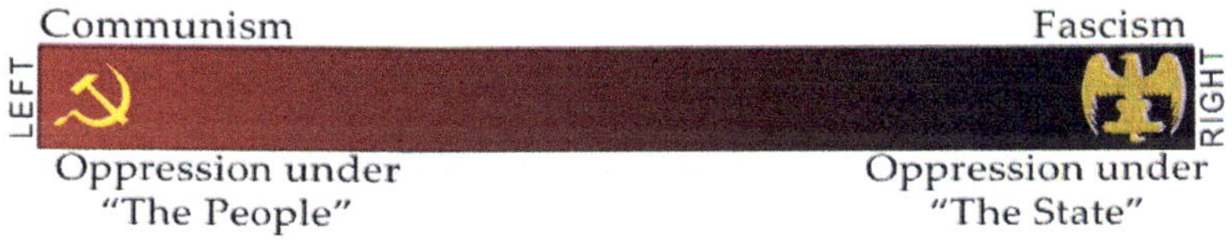

One might ask: Do these two "entities" actually exist? Are they not just slightly different oppressive political systems enacted by a few to control and rule over "the masses"?

Where does democracy or a government based on human rights fit on this spectrum? Are we to accept they fit somewhere between these two oppressive systems as many of the political charts illustrate?

Or is there more to this spectrum?

It becomes clear that the *traditional* political spectrum was crudely based on a dichotomy formed of two warring philosophies with a sloppy attempt to throw all other systems somewhere in between or ignore them completely.

What of the individual; the citizen, the "ruled"?

When you stand back and look at the various political systems from the viewpoint of the man on the street, the housewife, the worker, the artist, the religious person; what is government's relationship to them?

Should those in government serve the individual or does the individual exist to serve those in government?

Under communism, a person is made dependent on the government for his survival.

The U.S. government was designed to encourage and support independence.

From these two perspectives, a better dichotomy begins to present itself:

Dependence vs. Independence

This dichotomy begins to take in more of the political spectrum than the dichotomy of Communism vs. Fascism.

Dependence is not an absolute or unnatural state. Children are dependent upon their parents. Most grow to become independent adults, though some through injury, birth defect, or developmental disorder may never realize any real independence.

As a person grows older, he once again may become dependent upon others. But it cannot be denied that *independence* is a more natural and preferred condition for intelligent and able individuals.

Not understanding this may be a basic cause of the conflict between teenagers and their parents. Parents are understandably reluctant to give up control over their seemingly too young child, while young teens start feeling the need to establish control over their own lives.

Independence is associated with liberty and freedom. The definition of Freedom is *unrestricted action.*

But total freedom – a complete and total unrestricted action – is unworkable when the individual is a member of society. If he takes his neighbor's car without permission, what will happen as a result? Laws are put in place to protect the neighbor from such "unrestricted action". Society cannot exist without restrictions.

In an ideal society, these restrictions are naturally self-imposed. Self-governing is based on recognizing that one's neighbor has the same rights as oneself.

We each have a right to private property. But when these rights are violated, laws are written to stop "criminal" behavior. The crime being, really, an infringement upon the rights of another or his personal property.

Knowing and living by human rights provides a person with the freedom to act in their day-to-day activities, to pursue their own goals and happiness. As mentioned, this would be self-governing, perhaps the highest level of "government" that can exist.

And so, Freedom (unrestricted action) has been established as the extreme first dichotomy of the political spectrum.

The opposite of "*unrestricted action*" might be "*all action determined and controlled by an external source, with no personal choice to participate*". This is a condition of enslavement. Servitude to a master who has "*unrestricted action*" to restrict his slave's behavior and ownership.

Enslavement has little to do with having failed to follow the laws of the land. Sudden shifts of political power can find a whole minority suddenly in this condition, or worse, death. It has occurred countless times in history.

And so, the dichotomy which appears to be most workable for the expanded political spectrum would be Freedom vs. Enslavement.

Dichotomy of Freedom vs. Enslavement

The extremes of government can then be envisioned as: A government which enslaves or oppresses its people and a government which is founded on human rights and promotes freedom for all.

And so, we begin our look at the Political Spectrum based on the dichotomy Freedom vs Enslavement.

How much freedom is possible within a free society?

What restrictions are necessary to ensure freedom for all?

And what would these restrictions be based on?

Chapter Three

Freedoms, Rights and Enslavement

There is a significant difference between Freedoms and Rights, but their existence depend on each other. This distinction can greatly assist one's understanding of the expanded political spectrum.

In human history, freedom has carried such a high value that men consider it worth dying for. It is a very powerful banner. "Give me liberty or give me death" is a battle cry against oppression.

As mentioned earlier, freedom is *unrestricted action.* And as it relates to society, you cannot strive for "freedom" and exclude personal responsibility.

Personal responsibility might best be understood by looking at what we call "inalienable rights." Which are rights that cannot be given or taken away by the possessor.

In other words, inalienable rights are the freedoms you are entitled to just for being here and being alive. Congratulations!

From the moment a person becomes cognizant of his inalienable rights, he also should recognize that these rights apply to *every* human being.

The moral action is to respect the rights of all other beings. Thus, one can see that human rights are a necessary self-imposed restriction on one's personal freedom. One shouldn't steal something that is the personal property of another. One shouldn't hinder another's free speech. One shouldn't attack another for his religious beliefs, etc.

When we see people violating these rights, this mentality is the essence of those things we find objectionable, such as the bully, the racist, the rapist, the thief, the murderer, etc.

Protecting human rights is not complex. It is either done or it isn't.

Forcing one's religious beliefs upon another is an example of violating another's human rights. Thus, we see objection and upset when any religion attempts to *force* its laws and beliefs on others.

The American Constitution sought to protect your religious rights by prohibiting government interference of religions. State religions, as seen in some modern countries, are notorious for violating freedom of religion.

Freedom of Speech, another human right, recognizes that you may attempt to *persuade* another through conversation and writing. You have a right to communicate.

You also have the right to argue or not accept another's communication. It goes both ways.

Thus, acts to force another to stop communicating would violate his right to speech, no matter how disagreeable one may find the message. By walking away, one can simply end an unwanted communication by enacting your own right not to receive it.

From these examples we see that Human Rights are the basic agreed upon restrictions on the idea of total Freedom.

"Personal responsibility" could be defined as the exercise and defense of one's rights and the recognition that these same rights pertain to every other individual, no matter their age, sex, race, culture, religion or political views. Thus, personal responsibility would include refraining from impinging upon the rights of others as well as assisting another to defend his rights.

Each of us has the responsibility to enforce human rights within our society.

A criminal who breaks into a home, knowingly violates the rights of those who live there. He is ignoring his personal responsibility.

Society responds to such offenses with justice.

Criminal actions that violate the rights of others result in certain rights of the criminal's being forfeited. Specifically, he loses his right to participate in the activities of society by being locked up. He may even lose his right to life at the hands of a protective homeowner if he acts against these rights.

Freedom is unrestricted action. It is an unobtainable absolute the moment you interact with another sentient being, at which time one must "govern" oneself.

If a person governs himself, no further government is necessary. If a person does not act accordingly, "government" is then created by society to "protect" rights through justice and enforcement.

Self-governance, when practiced by a society, represents the highest form of government. It requires individuals who understand and respect the inalienable rights of others without need for force or oversight. In practical terms, this would operate through a minimal constitutional framework, similar to the U.S. Constitution, where government's purpose is protecting individual rights when violated.

Under such a system, citizens handle most disputes through voluntary means: arbitration, mediation, or civil courts. Government intervention occurs only when an individual's rights are clearly violated and voluntary resolution fails, or when protection from external threats is needed. This requires an educated populace. Laws remain minimal, focused solely on preventing rights violations rather than regulating behavior.

As an example, during the Wild West period of the U.S., the first form of government was usually a sheriff. His job was to keep order and protect the rights of all. He was necessary because some failed to govern themselves. There was no other reason for his existence.

So, while Freedom is positioned at the extreme right of the political spectrum, we can see the extreme right of government would be self-governance based on an agreement of human rights. An ideal worth envisioning.

Now, Let's look at the extreme left of the Spectrum.

Enslavement, of course, is the condition of being a slave.

It is a person who is the "legal" property of another and is forced to obey them. Usually, a slave is not considered human, but property.

Throughout man's history, people have found themselves in slavery. This occurs either through force or through deceitful trickery.

What sane man, of his own free will, would become a slave?

In slavery, one's actions are reduced to a single self-determined choice: Pretend to give up one's inalienable rights or be punished, tortured or killed. I say "pretend" because, by definition, inalienable rights cannot be given away. They are yours if you are alive.

As an aside, it is worth pointing out that before millions of Jews could be slaughtered in

Germany, they first had to be viewed as soulless animals with no human rights.

The 18th century psychologist in Germany declared that man was an animal. This set the stage for the Holocaust. Like unwanted domestic animals, they were herded into cages, men, women and children, and slaughtered.

This is government at its absolute lowest, dropping below enslavement to the psychotic level of genocide or death. This level of degradation has been observed in both fascist and communist governments where genocide or imprisonment is used to eliminate political opposition or an unwanted minority.

It is an interesting contrast that individuals who see eye to eye with human rights have more courage, more joy and greater satisfaction in securing human rights for others than for themselves. We call such people "heroes" and "saints". We see them as great men. They willingly risk their own lives so others may live.

For those who would be dictators or slave masters, their greatest ambition is to secure "freedom" for themselves at the expense of others. Such people have no real joy, no satisfaction, and feel their own freedom requires that others should be enslaved. It is a sad and depraved condition. And when such people work their way into power, it is disastrous for society.

This is the dichotomy of Freedom vs. Enslavement. All political philosophies fit somewhere on the spectrum between these two extremes.

How do current political systems relate to this dichotomy?

Chapter Four

A Brief Look at Political and Economic Systems

Dichotomy of Freedom vs. Enslavement

This chapter provides a brief look at the various common political systems in use today. It also briefly covers several economic systems.

Democratic Republic

A democratic republic is founded on principles of Freedom and Human Rights for every individual. It is formed under a constitution which defines its functions and formation.

It is a state in which political power is held by the people and their elected representatives. It usually has an elected or nominated president rather than a monarch.

This form of government will be further explored in Chapter 7.

Free-Market

This is an economic system in which prices are determined by unrestricted competition between privately owned businesses.

The free market is a product-based system of exchange. In other words, something is created and sold to another who wishes to have it.

The value of a product depends upon what people are willing to pay. Scarcity and abundance can greatly affect the value of a product.

Barter

The origin of the free-market is the barter system: direct exchange of one product for another — such as a fish for some grain.

Bartering one item for another is a workable system but clumsy. A person must carry their product around to find someone who has what one wants and who is willing to trade it for what one has.

The solution to this clumsiness is money.

Coin-Based Monetary System

Coin was created to make trade easier. Silver, gold, or anything agreed upon, which holds a known value can act as "money". People have to have confidence that the money will maintain a certain value.

The monetary system simplifies other aspects of life.

When people sell their products, they use the money in several ways:

1. To buy items they must have for their survival, such as food and shelter.

2. Reinvestment the money for what is needed for future production.

3. Save some money for future needs and emergencies.

Savings, when they exceed what is required for the above three points, are referred to as **wealth**. This money could be used to raise one's standard of living, such as obtaining a larger house, travel or some luxury items.

Savings can also be used in a way that increases one's wealth. This is known as investing.

Investment

This leads us to the concept of Capitalism.

In the 12th and 13th centuries "capital" described merchandise, money and money lent with interest.

A **Capitalist** is a person who uses money to invest in trade and industry for profit, obtaining more money with the money invested.

Why does Capitalism get a bad name? Is there something destructive about it?

The answer is yes—but not all capitalism is destructive. There are two distinctly different forms of capitalism: constructive and destructive.

Constructive Capitalism supports private businesses and free-market production. Destructive Capitalism finances government operations and expansion, profiting from debt and taxation rather than production. This form puts governments at risk, becoming answerable to the investors rather than to the citizens. This distinction is vital to maintaining a free society.

Chapter 12 explores how destructive capitalism operates and why recognizing this difference is critical to identifying the true enemies of freedom.

Democracy

Democracy is the most misused word in politics.

You have likely heard many times that America is a democracy. This is not true. It is a Constitutional Republic. It uses democratic procedures but also includes a system to protect the inalienable rights of the minority.

Democracy, strictly speaking, is majority-rule; one person, one vote. The proposals which get the most votes become "law".

As an example, a group of men catch a person suspected of murder. Under democracy, a person might propose to string up the "murderer" on the nearest tree. Another suggests taking him in for a trial. If the majority agrees with the first man, there's a hanging, guilty or not.

That is democracy by definition. It could be viewed as "mob rule". It does not promise justice or human rights.

There is something about mob-rule that everyone recognizes as irrational, especially when it is based on fear, hate and anger.

In contrast, the U.S. Constitution protects the individual or a minority group from unjust democratic procedures and it provides a system of appeal if an individual feels his rights have been violated.

Democratic Socialism

This is the lowest level of democracy. The majority are convinced that the profits and wealth earned by an individual do not really belong to him but should be taken and given to those who cannot or will not work.

Since "the rich" are always a minority, they would have no recourse to keep the wealth they worked for.

One of the reasons you see the standard of living collapse in socialist countries is that those who can work, quit working or leave. This system has repeatedly failed to raise the poor out of poverty, but in fact, eventually, drastically increases the number of poor.

When you reward those who do not work, you get more people who will not work.

"From each according to his ability, to each according to his need." This is the guiding socialist slogan.

How does a free society get reduced to the level of socialism?

There is a very precise method used by those who wish to create a socialist society. It is something that should be known. It is very much in play in our societies today. This vital information is covered in Chapter 8 under the sub-section of Democratic Socialism.

Fascism

This is an authoritarian form of government under the control of a dictator, allowing no political opposition (especially communism), forcibly suppressing dissent, and rigidly controlling industrial and economic activities.

Fascism often comes about as a direct response to communist and socialist influences upon a society.

Fascism usually promises to move a country back toward freedom and a free-market economy. But because of its militant activity to suppress all opposition, society is further splintered by injustices and reduced human rights.

Businesses may experience an increase in freedom and prosperity, but these freedoms are usually as granted by The State and have no guarantees, being at the whim of the current or succeeding dictator.

Communism

This is a form of government which takes ownership of <u>all</u> **capital** of a country, that is to say, the government controls all means of production, distribution of products and goods, and the manner in which products are exchanged.

This, in fact, includes the ownership of the individual. Each person becomes the property of *"The People"* or really, the Communist Party.

As in fascism, there is no allowance for political opposition. There is complete control by the ruling party with total obedience expected by citizens who are made completely dependent upon government.

The individual owns nothing. He obtains what he needs by requests through local agencies. When a requested item becomes available it is provided "free".

Buying things, such as a needed appliance would be against the law; no one owns property because it all belongs to "the People".

If any form of free market exists, it operates as a "Black Market" and is considered criminal activity.

Black Market

This is the illegal sale and distribution of officially controlled commodities. In the United States, drugs are sold on the black market. In a communist country, food, appliances, etc., if not obtained through official lines, is bought and sold on the black market.

Anarchy

This is not a form of government but either a complete collapse of government resulting in chaos, or it is a very high level of self-rule, requiring no oversight. These two forms will be further discussed and clarified in the Subsection on Anarchy in Chapter 8.

With these brief descriptions you are now familiar with the various political systems.

What makes political systems on the far left and far right a dichotomy?

How can political system be completely opposite from each other and what does that mean?

Chapter Five
Boundaries of the Political Spectrum

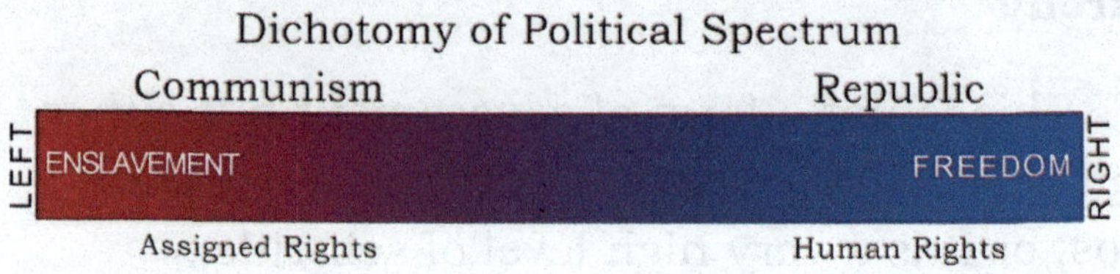

The Far Right: In the *expanded* political spectrum, the ideal Republic would be organized around the protection of inalienable rights of individuals, families, groups, and would support and forward human rights for its citizens and humanity.

The United States Constitution attempted to form such a government. Though not a perfect solution it was a considerable step toward freedom and human rights.

The Far Left: Within the most complex and confusing political spectrum charts previously created, the left side has always been occupied by communism. And it will be seen that communism does occupy the left most position on the spectrum. It is the dichotomy of the ideal republic.

"Equality for all" replaces the concept of human rights for all.

Enforcing "equality" on society does not make people equal. The action of forcing a person to be equal to another in any way violates his human rights.

Socialism (everything owned by "the people" (the communist party) and nothing owned by the individual replaces the Free Market.

The concept that you own everything as "the people" but own nothing is a twisted mockery of the free market. Try borrowing the Chairman's car for the night. After all, it is yours too, isn't it? But atlas, you are not quite that equal.

The barbed-wire fences that have been constructed around communist countries in the past existed to stop the populace from escaping, not to prevent illegal immigration into the country.

Again, one might imagine more slavish conditions than are found in a communist-controlled country, but for now it will serve as the anchor at the far left of the political spectrum.

And so, we begin with these new opposing political systems: Communism vs. a Republic.

Are they really so different as to be completely opposite?

Dichotomy of Political Spectrum

It was fascinating to study the opposing relationships between these two political systems.

What is legal or considered desirable in one of these systems, is despised or illegal in the other. It is hard to imagine such differences in human governance and thought. But these differences exist.

Remember, there are as many variations of communism as there are communist leaders. These comparisons are based on the tenants of communism as proposed by Karl Marx and Vladimir Lenin whose writings are later referenced.

Let's look at some of these differences. The terms Left and Right are used for simplification.

On the Right, buying and selling on the free market is normal commerce; on the Left, this same activity is considered illegal black-market activity.

Buying and selling anything under communist philosophy violates the concept of non-ownership and is therefore illegal. The seller has no right to sell it (because it belongs to The People, and the buyer has no right to buy it because he already "owns" it by being "the people".

On the Right there would be many privately owned *news* outlets. This is expected and is considered vital as it provides a variety of viewpoints. Some of these news outlets may take on the role of watchdogs against government misconduct. You see that with a growing number of independent news outlets and commentators in the U.S., countering the corporate media loaded with political bias toward the left.

No matter what subject is published, it is protected from government persecution. This is known as Freedom of the Press.

On the Left, there is a single government-operated source of news. Its "press" serves to relay the party-accepted viewpoint of current events. The press is not news but government-controlled propaganda. There is no dissenting voice allowed. There is no Freedom of the Press.

Freedom of Speech represents the free flow of *ideas*, with no restrictions. The value of free speech cannot be underestimated in its positive effect on the creativity, productivity and achievements of a society.

On the far left, exercising free speech, if not aligned with government propaganda, can result in imprisonment, torture or death. This is where the concept of political correctness comes from. The Right has no regard for political correctness.

Honesty vs Dishonesty

A basic doctrine of communism is “The ends justify the means.” A party member not only can lie, cheat and deceive but is expected too, if it is necessary, to forward the party’s objectives. The individual’s ability to succeed through any form of deception is held in high esteem.

In a free society, honesty, truth and openness of one’s intentions are expected. If one discovered otherwise in a person, their reputation would be ruined. A dishonest person is not likely to be trusted again. A man’s worth is only as great as his word.

The Left sees these higher ideals as a weakness of the Right, and to be taken advantage of.

A free society has consistently resulted in prosperity. Creativity, productivity, quality, innovation, and individuality are all part and parcel of a free society.

It is hard to keep good people in a state of destitution. It can only be done by stamping out individuality, by rewarding non-production and penalizing production.

The Right, not understanding the complete opposite mentality of honesty vs. dishonesty, truth vs. lies, openness vs. deceit, quickly becomes the victim of communist plotting and planning.

No honest and decent person would consider that a person could have such a twisted mentality, and his only error, and eventual downfall, would be in failing to detect lies and dishonesty where they exist.

Usually, the first evidence that such covert activities are taking place is whether living conditions are getting better or getting worse for the individual, family and groups and could extend to all of mankind.

Grasp that concept. Usually, the only evidence that such covert activities are taking place is whether conditions are getting better or getting worse. Look for these specific indicators:

Are people becoming more or less literate? Are families stronger or more fractured? Is drug addiction rising or falling? Are people becoming more productive or more dependent? Is the standard of living improving or declining? Are individual rights expanding or contracting? Is public discourse becoming more honest or more deceptive?

When money and attention increase in an area, but conditions worsen, corruption or sabotage is likely at work.

For example, is the education system in America getting better or worse?

Despite the ever-increasing attention and money that flows to correct and improve education, statistics show education is worsening.

Is mental health getting better or worse? Research the connection between psychiatric medications and both suicide rates and incidents of mass violence. When "solutions" correlate with worsening conditions, question whether they are solutions at all.

Are crippling, suicide-inducing mind-altering drugs really a solution? If so, why are most (if not all) mass shooters found to have been on these drugs?

If these drugs really help, why did an average of twenty veterans commit suicide each day after the Iraq War?

Real solutions in areas such as education and mental health would result in improving conditions. Things would be getting better, not worse.

People in a free society naturally have little, if any interest in people who wish to follow communist doctrine. Those who freely choose to live under such arrangements would have the right and freedom to do so if their beliefs were not forced upon others.

On the other hand, communists see a free society as a system which is as unnatural as fire on water. And with all evidence, they act to destroy it. The left isn't satisfied to just live under their own system of communism but feel they must enforce it upon the rest of the world, and they actively work to do so.

It may be difficult to accept this dichotomy, but as in all of man's games and wars, there is always an opposing team. And if one team is much stronger than the other, then the weaker side, if they want to win, must keep their identity, intentions and strategies hidden. It must operate in a well-organized if deceitful manner. And it must find and use its enemy's weaknesses against him.

Without understanding the covert actions which a weaker foe may take, a free society is in danger of losing its freedom without understanding how or why.

Remember, we are looking at the extreme ends of a spectrum.

How many people are capable of, and want to live in a truly free society?

On the other hand, how many people are so insane as to strike out against a free society just because it is free. And then work tirelessly and covertly to destroy it?

Chapter Six

The decline of Political Systems

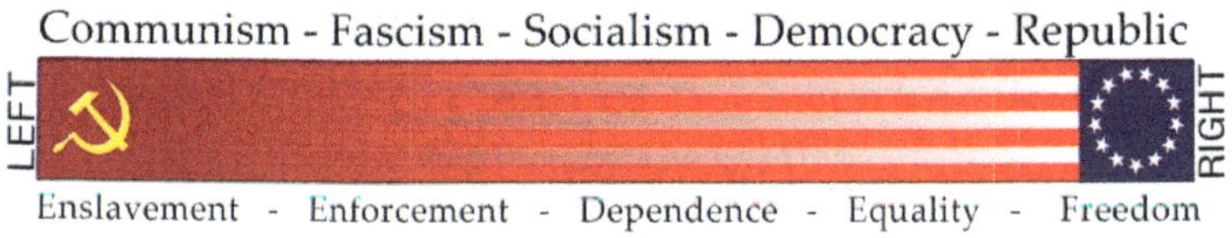

The dichotomy of slavery and freedom allows one to envision a progression from the highest levels of freedom toward a complete loss of individual freedom: a loss of independence, a loss of personal liberty, decay of individual responsibility, loss of spirituality, loss of ownership, productivity and a loss of real, trusting camaraderie with one's fellow man.

Each progressive step from right to left brings about a state of mind in the individual where, either his desire for the above qualities diminish, replaced perhaps, with the desire for personal or financial security; or with increase intensity in his attitude to defend liberty, which taken to a desperate extreme, results in the destruction of those who would enslave.

There are many variations of the major governmental systems in use today. They are not set in stone.

Just as with the infinity of colors in the spectrum of the rainbow, political systems can take on many forms on the spectrum.

And as with colors, there can be an endless number of names used to describe the various political systems. The reason for any confusion regarding any political system has been the lack of a sufficiently broad spectrum on which to place it and from which one can compare it to the others.

As an example, under fascism you would find a variety of names such as Nationalism, Nazism, Totalitarianism, Dictatorship, etc. These terms are often used to define each other. None are exactly like the other, but you could examine their relationship to freedom and accurately place them upon the political spectrum.

The matter is complicated by the level of wisdom and benevolence (or lack thereof) shown by a particular leader under any one of these systems, resulting in shifts toward the left or right of the spectrum under his leadership.

For instance, the government of China has moved toward the right from communism toward fascism by embracing free-market activity and private ownership, while maintaining rigid dictatorial control over dissenters.

China's intense buildup of military is very characteristic of fascism. The road from enslavement back toward freedom is a very difficult and dangerous road for a government and its leaders. It has rarely, if ever been done without bloodshed, not because it cannot be done, but because these leaders lack an understanding of the actual political spectrum and thus have no clear path back toward freedom for their citizens. Of course, they would have to desire freedom for their country first, which is a rare characteristic on the Left.

Conversely, countries like Canada and modern Germany have drifted left from their more freedom-oriented roots, implementing increasingly socialist policies while maintaining democratic processes. Japan, despite significant government involvement in industry, has maintained enough free-market activity to remain prosperous, though its position has shifted over decades.

Men can, and have, lived under many systems of government. But where government becomes oppressive, eventually men rise and deliver a blow to those (possibly once entrusted) leaders who became apparent traitors to their citizens. Often anarchy may follow. But once violent revolt has occurred, if the new leaders lack an understanding of the political spectrum and the various government systems, they often walk the country further to the left and life becomes even more difficult.

This has been the history of civilizations.

There is a constant struggle between good and evil — only the left insists there is no such thing as evil (except when they use it as a weapon against their political rivals.)

The majority of any populace is made up of productive and decent people. However, a very small minority of insane people view good as evil and evil as good.

They secretly work towards the destruction of what exists. They hate the very thought of freedom and liberty. And because they are such a small minority, their covert activity often goes undetected by the majority until their actions have brought about decay and turmoil in society.

You will encounter a few of these characters in later chapters. It is important that you are able to recognize their methods, only then can you avoid falling victim to them. When you uncover their methods and motives, they become ineffective. After all, they are a minority; and they are insane.

Even good leaders can make mistakes. Their actions are magnified because they affect so many. A good measuring tool to evaluate a leader is this: Is life becoming more orderly and easier to live? Or are anger, upset and division occurring, interrupting the lives of more and more people?

Many Germans trusted and loved what Hitler promised for their country. Some, however, saw through the talk and observed the actions. His intentions and actions finally brought destruction to all of Europe, including a miserable conclusion for their homeland.

Free nations must always be aware and assume there is an active force working to bring down a freedom-based society. It may be completely incomprehensible that this is true. But history supports it. It would be very wise to investigate areas of society where conditions are worsening and determine who is suppressing those areas and get them out of government.

Look how rapidly the U.S. education system deteriorated.

Look at how the U.S. manufacturing capability was greatly reduced.

If free people ignore such worsening conditions, they will find their country sliding across the spectrum from right to left, with life becoming more and more difficult and the country becoming more and more divided.

The following two chapters should provide sufficient information on each political system to gain a very good grasp of where each lay on the spectrum of Freedom vs Enslavement.

Chapter Seven

A Constitutional Republic

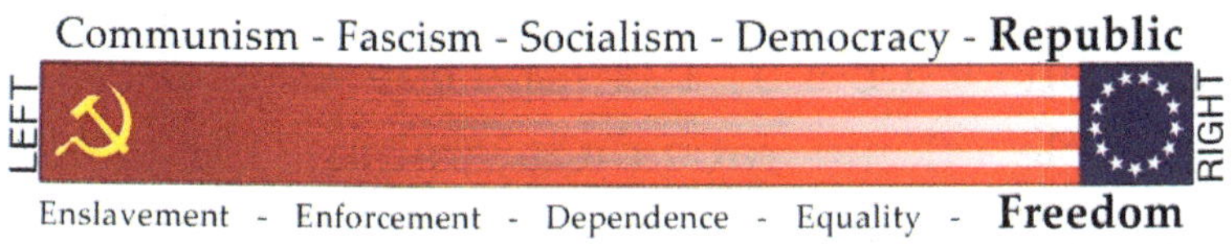

What is a Constitutional Republic?

Unfortunately, there are few people who can accurately answer that question.

If you, as an American, cannot immediately answer that question with certainty, it should alarm and dismay you.

One of the reasons for the confusion and uncertainty is that different forms of government have called themselves a republic.

For instance, in the latter part of the 20th century there was the *Union of Soviet Socialist Republics (USSR).*

There is the current *People's Republic of China.*

Both governments were formed out of communist revolution. Both are quite different from each other and neither stands up to the dictionary definition of a republic.

When Mao proclaimed the People's Republic of China on October 1, 1949, he characterized it as a "people's democratic dictatorship". The concept of “democracy” applied only to those who supported the communist effort. The “dictatorship” applied to anyone opposed to the new socialist state. In other words, you went along with the communist party on your own choice, or you were forced to go along with it.

And then there is the United States of America, a republic which closely fits the definition. It too was formed out of the ashes of a revolution.

What makes this American republic different from the others?

The basic description of a *Republic* found in dictionaries is that the power of a country is held by *the people* and their chosen representatives. But these definitions omit an essential element which defines the uniqueness of the American republic: *that the individual has control of his own life and fortunes.*

The Declaration of Independence, U.S. Constitution and the Bill of Rights are the foundation of the United States Republic. They proclaim and support the idea that all men are born with unalienable rights granted by the Creator and are considered equal under the law.

The Declaration of Independence defines the American purpose and spirit. It is indisputably the true “American Dream”.

The Constitution represents an effort to create a form of government capable of achieving the concepts of freedom laid out in the Declaration of Independence.

The Bill of Rights boldly, clearly and without reservation restricts those in government from infringing upon the unalienable rights of honest Americans.

It is more accurately the *Bill of Government Restrictions.*

We often hear the American Dream is to own a home, create one’s own business, or become rich. Though these may be desirable objectives, they are really nothing more than potential achievements made possible by the application of the principles of a free society.

The American Dream would be best expressed as; an individual having the freedom and opportunity to pursue his dreams, whatever they may be, as long as they do not infringe upon the natural freedoms and rights of another. Just as government can become oppressive or destructive, so could an individual or a group.

The U.S. government's purpose is implementing the Founding Documents *toward* protecting human rights for each citizen. The second purpose is to protect the country from external forces and internal enemies who act against these two purposes.

The United States' republic was unique, because its founders and leaders were not men motivated by power and self-interest. Like most people, they were involved in the pursuit of happiness, until it was interrupted by the actions of an oppressive government.

Where communist leaders rose to be masters of their populations, the U.S. founding fathers refused to take on that role. They served as elected leaders and then stepped aside to live in freedom amongst their fellow Americans.

Instead of grabbing and holding the power gained by the Revolutionary War, these leaders forged two vessels in which the power would be enshrined and locked away from tyrannical hands. Nestled within these two vessels are the power and freedoms of the people of the United States.

These two vessels are the *Constitution* and the *Bill of Rights*, both based on the ideals envisioned in the *Declaration of Independence.*

It is not enough that these documents sit in Washington D.C. to be viewed by those who visit them. They should be visible and objects of interest in our homes, schools and higher educational systems.

The only vault which guarantees the safety of the contents of these two vessels is not a shrine in Washington DC, but the hearts and minds of each American and their future generations.

Mass ignorance of these documents is the only way we could lose what was fought for and created; how can a person continue to uphold something he is unaware of nor understands?

"The people made the Constitution, and the people can unmake it. It is the creature of their will, and lives only by their will." Chief Justice John Marshall, 1821

Your Republic consists of the concepts laid down in these three rare documents. Lose them, fail to understand them, fail to educate every generation on them, and you lose the republic so bravely fought for; so caringly and intelligently forged to guarantee freedom and equality for all men.

The Declaration of Independence, written prior to the American Revolution, gives compelling reason and justification for the revolution's existence. It further defined the purpose of government and laid the basis of its formation:

"We hold these truths to be self-evident, that all men are created equal, that they are endowed by their Creator with certain unalienable Rights; that among these are Life, Liberty and the pursuit of Happiness.

"That to secure these rights, Governments are instituted among Men, deriving their just powers from the consent of the governed,

"That whenever any Form of Government becomes destructive to these ends, it is the Right of the People to alter or to abolish it, and to institute new Government, laying its foundation on such principles and organizing its powers in such form as to them shall seem most likely to affect their Safety and Happiness."

Following the Revolutionary War, a new government was established based on these principles of freedom, and it was organized to prevent their violation.

"We the People of the United States, in Order to form a more perfect Union, to establish Justice, ensure domestic Tranquility, provide for the common defense, promote the general Welfare, and secure the Blessings of Liberty to ourselves and our Posterity, do ordain and establish this Constitution for the United States of America." The Constitution of the United States

When the Constitution was adopted, a number of State Representatives expressed a desire for an additional document which would declare government limitations. They wanted a guarantee which would prevent misinterpretation and abuse of Federal powers.

The result was the first ten amendments to the Constitution, which became known as the Bill of Rights (which perhaps could have been more accurately called the "Bill of Government Restrictions.") Its purpose was not to codify all inalienable rights, but to declare restrictions upon the Federal Government, to prevent infringement upon the freedoms and rights of the States and the people.

Basic freedoms such as Religion, Speech and the Press were areas which government was expressly prohibited from infringing upon.

The right to bear arms, and to be secure from unreasonable search and seizure, were other explicit restrictions placed upon the Federal Government.

The Bill of Rights also stated that just because certain rights were named within the document, did not indicate that other unnamed rights were not retained by the people or the States, a sort of catch-all phrase.

The Bill was not intended to be a list of all human rights, but rather to lay down the principle that the unalienable rights of man were not to be infringed upon by those who were temporarily handed the power to govern.

These three documents laid out the formation of the United States Republic.

There have been seventeen additional amendments to the Constitution. Some have furthered the cause of freedom, such as the Thirteenth Amendment, which made it a crime to enslave another person.

On the other hand, some amendments have reduced the freedoms and rights of the individual, such as the sixteenth amendment, which gave the Federal Government the power to tax an individual's income.

The founding fathers severely frowned upon and fought against the idea of an income tax.

To make matters worse, (but was part of the overall scheme behind this Sixteenth Amendment), was the immediate creation of the Internal Revenue Service to collect taxes. Then followed the formation of the Federal Reserve. All within a year.

Who was behind these bills? This subversion of the Constitution is covered in more detail in Chapter 12.

How does democracy relate to our republic?

The Founders created a system where State Governments (Elected leaders of each State) and *qualified* members of the populace, would select the leaders and representatives of the Federal Government.

Not everyone was considered qualified to cast a vote. This is an important distinction between a Republic and a Democracy.

Our Republic was designed to escape the instability of democracy.

Our founding fathers understood that majority rule was injurious to personal freedoms. The individual is always at the mercy of the group in a democracy.

However, did the founding fathers have the foresight to see other potential dangers to the republic?

What are the signs that freedom is fading?

What happens when people lose sight of the purposes laid out in the Declaration of Independence?

A decaying Republic slowly drifts away from freedom toward the left side of the political spectrum.

What does a Republic descend into?

Chapter Eight

Democracy through Communism

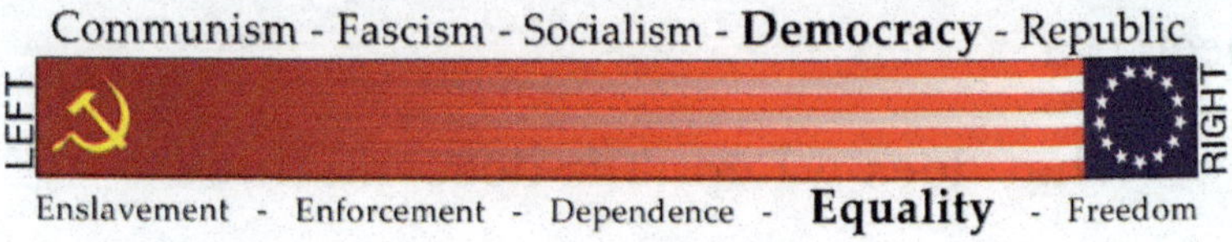

It has been said that Thomas Jefferson was the father of Democracy. It is true that Thomas Jefferson felt government should be "of by and for the people". However, it is highly inaccurate to label him as a champion of democracy. He would likely laugh at you.

Perhaps all that needs to be said about democracy has already been said by Jefferson and others who have rejected it as a form of government. Democracy: 'majority rule", becomes a very unstable state of affairs. The flaws of democracy are obvious in the writings found on both sides of the spectrum.

To supporters of freedom, democracy limits the rights of the minority.

In contrast, those who despise freedom, have found democracy to be an effective tool to drag a free society down.

"Democracy is two wolves and a lamb voting on what to have for lunch. Liberty is a well-armed lamb contesting the vote."

Benjamin Franklin

"A democracy is nothing more than mob rule, where 51% of the people may take away the rights of the other 49%."

Thomas Jefferson

"Remember, democracy never lasts long. It soon wastes, exhausts, and murders itself. There never was a democracy yet that did not commit suicide."

John Adams

Democracy is positioned just to the left of a democratic republic on the political spectrum.

There is still a good deal of freedom within a democracy. However, as clearly covered in the above quotes, freedom and rights can be determined by the majority and any minority is at risk of losing their rights.

If our founding fathers rejected democracy as a form of government, how is it that we think of and refer to our country as a democracy?

Politicians say it constantly. The media says it consistently. And we all seem to agree that we are a great democracy.

However, when we pledge allegiance, we do so "to the Republic".

It would be necessary and the first objective of those who opposed freedom, to move a republic toward a democracy.

Has there been any alteration of our election system from that which was intended by our founding fathers to prevent majority rule? The answer is yes.

The Constitution lays out an election system you would not recognize.

If you study the Constitution you will discover that the electoral system is based on a democratic procedure which has the purpose of protecting against majority rule.

1. *"The House of Representatives shall be chosen by the people." (This body represents the people's rights)*
2. *"The Senate shall be chosen by the Legislature of each State." (This body was intended to represent the States rights)*
3. *"The executive Power shall be vested in a President of the United States of America. Elected by State Appointed Electors".*

The election of the president was intended to be out of the direct hands of both the States and the Populace.

The beauty of this system is that the elected officials in each of the three bodies (House, Senate and Presidency) would have their own interests, coming from three separate sources (the people, the States and an educated class) which would have the foresight to select the most qualified candidate for the Executive Branch.

With this system, the guard against majority rule was in place. Democratic procedure was in use but democracy as "majority rule" was not.

What still remains of our republic? How far has the country slid left into democracy?

The year 1913 was terrible for the Constitution, the Republic and the American people. One of the several major changes that occurred in this infamous year was the

Seventeenth Amendment. It altered point #2 above to this:

"The Senate shall also be chosen ***by the people."***

The States no longer had their interests and rights represented. The Republic with that change moved a big step toward democracy.

The excuses used by those who spearheaded this amendment were corruption and deadlock in various State legislations which left senate seats unassigned for months.

If corruption and deadlock existed at State levels, the solution would have been for the States to **a.** Arrest the corrupt politicians and get them replaced with honest people and **b.** come up with a solution at the State level which would resolve deadlocks. But most likely b. would have been unnecessary once a. was done.

This destructive public relations "solution" did nothing effective to address the so-called problems at State level, but simply "by-passed" and altered the Constitution, taking the Republic toward a democracy.

Who was behind this? Progressive reformers of the early 1900s, including members of the Progressive Party and populist democrats, championed this amendment. Key advocates included Senator Joseph Bristow of Kansas (who introduced the resolution), William Jennings Bryan, and Robert La Follette. These "Progressives" promoted the false idea of "equality" through direct democracy, arguing that

State legislatures were corrupt and unresponsive to "the people."

The amendment was ratified in 1913 — the same year that saw the Federal Reserve Act (creation of the Federal Reserve) and the 16th Amendment (income tax). This convergence was not coincidental.

Their actual intention was to move the country toward a direct democracy which would eventually, naturally, deteriorate into a democratic socialism, the next step to the left.

If a republic fails to correct itself and reestablish itself, when necessary, the country will surely slide into democracy and forget that it ever was a republic.

Under democracy, minority groups begin to lose their rights and freedoms. The rights and freedoms of various religious, racial or economic groups can become targets of attack by the majority.

Individuals who have the ability to be executives (those who can organize and create production) are few. Such people thrive and are celebrated in a republic and free-market system and often become wealthy. They set an example of what can be achieved.

In a democracy, such people, being a minority, can eventually be made the target of propaganda designed to create a jealous malcontent "majority".

The leader of the Fascist Party also recognized the flaws of democracy.

> ***Fascism rejects the notion that the majority, by the simple fact that it is a majority, can direct human society. Fascism affirms the unchanging, "beneficial and fruitful inequality of mankind". Not all men are created equally and thus should not be made the same through some mere operation of a mechanical process such as the right to vote.***
>
> Benito Mussolini
>
> (Paraphrased for clarity, see full and exact quote in Reference section)

Fascism's solution of course, is a dictatorship. A whole different ball game covered later in the chapter on fascism.

If a society under a democratic system does not last, toward what form of government is it heading?

The answer to this question is quite correctly revealed in the writings of Karl Marx, Father of Communism: ***"Democracy is the road to socialism."***

This conclusion can be supported by the fact and evidence that in a democracy, a certain class of politician begin to make promises to the working men (always a majority in any country) to enact certain benefits or handouts from government.

Modern Western European countries like Sweden and Norway fall between democracy and democratic socialism on this spectrum. While citizens enjoy considerable personal freedom and prosperity built on earlier free-market foundations, high taxation and extensive government programs have moved these nations leftward. Their position demonstrates that movement on the spectrum is gradual, not sudden.

The political promises start out subtly at first, but eventually, such promises become more pronounced until the idea of taking money from the rich and redistributing it through social programs becomes a campaign slogan.

It is interesting to note that in a democracy, education of children reduces to a system. All students are required to go through this "educational" system.

Group education misses the individual who is slower and also fails to engage the student who is brighter. The curriculum begins to support certain political views and opinions.

Education moves toward learning data, rather than learning to think and evaluate data. The average intelligence of the students appears to drop and thus "standards" are dropped. And the downward spiral continues.

In a democracy, left-leaning activist groups or vested interests can, through public relations campaigns and concerted use of the Press, create antagonism toward various minorities or sectors of society.

The energy sector of a society often falls prey to such attacks. Religion, which works to uphold the moral standards of a society, often becomes a target of these attacks. Not as a whole, but wherever intolerance can be created between various religious groups or sects, a wedge is inserted and the decay continues.

Wealthy people, "the rich", eventually become a target. Criticism is leveled at this minority as "not doing their part", "not contributing their fair share" or "taking advantage of the people through outrageous profits". The attackers never care that most of these people are the very ones keeping society productive and prosperous.

The Press in a democracy starts to become a tool for the enemies of freedom to attack certain minorities. The Press begins to sing the praises of government regulation as necessary to overcome the problems of society.

Those who raise a voice or attempt to resist the slide from a republic to a democracy are called old fashioned, conservative, outdated, out of touch and in any number of ways isolated as "different from" or out of agreement with the "majority" of society and said to be in the minority, when in truth they are still the majority.

But because of these attacks, more and more become silent.

In a democracy, you just need 51% of the society feeling strongly enough about the "evils" of some group's actions (or the Press reporting that such is the case) and that group can be unjustly attacked, and its rights reduced.

As the unworkability of democracy becomes a burden on society, the government proposes even more "solutions" to the problems facing society: more regulations, more taxes, more controls on businesses.

The government also begins to take over sectors of society, such as transportation and utilities. Thus, one sees society spiraling down.

What does a democracy decay into?

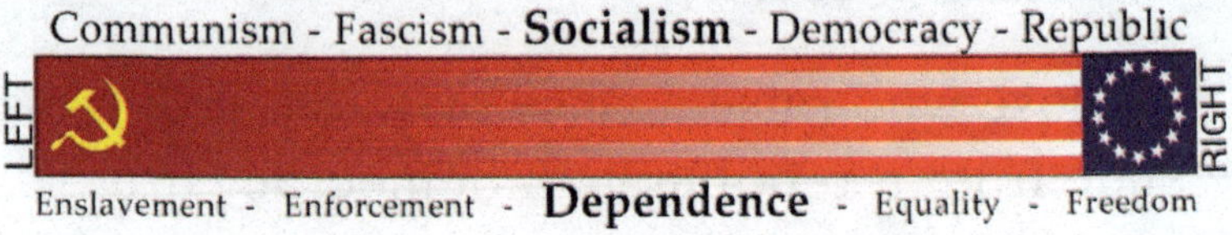

Democratic Socialism

- A political and economic theory of social organization that advocates that the means of production, distribution, and exchange should be owned or regulated by the community as a whole.

- A transitional social state between the overthrow of capitalism and the realization of communism.

It is really the beginning of the overthrow of the free market, not necessarily capitalism, as will be explained and demonstrated in a later chapter.

Where socialist economics may have some workability with a small community with a common goal or purpose, such as one may find in some religious orders, it becomes very unworkable in a vast and diverse cultural scene such as a State or country.

In a deteriorating society, socialism is the means by which government increases its control over society and by so doing reduces the power and freedoms of the individual.

The following quote from Karl Marx is the key to understanding the communist system of bringing down a free society: ***"Democracy is the road to Socialism."***

Why would the Father of Communism be interested in bringing a free society to socialism?

Because Marx understood that a free republic would never accept socialism. Why should they?

But with the right public relations (propaganda) programs, people could be made to accept democracy as being a "faire", more inclusive system.

"Disenfranchisement" is one of the key words for those seeking a democracy. After all, people want their vote to count.

Only when the republic sinks into democracy could it then be pulled down into socialism, which is the next milestone toward communism.

What Socialism begins (government takeover of major private companies such as utilities, transportation, communications, energy, etc.), Communism finishes with a complete takeover of all capital and labor of a country.

Democracy is the embryo of communism, socialism is the fetus, fascism is the pain of labor and communism is the attempt to provide for and keep its unruly and ungrateful children under its control — forever.

In a socialist environment, the artist is rewarded and promoted for degraded and meaningless art. “Pop” artists stretch the bounds of good taste and set odd examples for children in the society. Yet they are gushed over by the media and its critics.

Art becomes a tool for propaganda for changing the values and viewpoints of society. Certain groups are stereotyped and presented over and over again until they are actually viewed as such.

An example of this is the American father in TV and movies. He is usually portrayed as childish, stupid and selfish. Show after show on TV present men in a degraded state where women need to take control and bring order.

And it eventually starts to become a reality.

Education in a socialist country is heavily combined with propaganda. Students are educated in the value and goodness of government and the evils of corporations and the selfishness of the rich. These are common messages through a young person's life. "Free education for all!" "Cancel student debt!" "The evil rich!"

In education, the idea is introduced that children must develop strong self-esteem to be successful. This only builds a weak, selfish culture. Whereas in a free republic, emphasis would be on developing a high level of personal responsibility, not just for self, but for one's roll in life and one's fellow man.

In a Democratic Socialism, the Press is dominated with voices forwarding the ideas of a socialistic society (though this would have been the case far before the society ever fell to this depth) making it seem more agreed upon than it actually is.

Socialistic Press forwards any idea which supports more government takeover. They strongly believe their actions are necessary to help transform society into what they believe is the ideal for the country. Articles attack those who stand up for a country based on freedom.

One could say, based on this spectrum, that Socialism would then be the road to fascism, and it would be a true statement. But there's an interesting twist at this part of the spectrum. And one that brings fear to the socialist and communists.

Societies change very slowly. The impulse toward freedom is very strong and not easily nullified.

Some members of society who become aware of the erosion of their natural freedoms, especially when they cannot spot the true cause of the decline, can become fearful and angry in their attempt to protest the decay they observe. This anger is often flamed by the way they are portrayed by socialist media.

The Tea Party, started in the first decade of this century, is a perfect example. This movement had a purpose to increase the understanding of and to reduce the growing infringement by government on the natural rights of its citizens.

Individuals in this group objected to such socialistic programs as The Fair Health Act, or better known as Obama Care, a program which moved the finances of health care insurance under the control of government.

Also, public unrest occurs because of worsening economic conditions which naturally follow the implementation of more and more socialist policies.

The government begins to take on huge debt under the strain of supporting so many who are not producing (even though they continue to blame their own failures on "capitalism" and the evils of the "Right".)

As conditions continue to worsen, people begin to look for something, someone, through whatever means, to get government under control and to regain their freedoms.

Eventually, a leader will arise, who will fearlessly speak out against the evils of the politicians, the Press and will attack them on the terrible conditions these establishments have brought about.

If socialism and communism are recognized as the problem, they will come under attack. Promises are made to return the country to a free economy. This results in a powerful surge in those who wish to move their country back toward the right of the spectrum.

If this leader truly recognizes and acknowledges the purposes and intentions of the Declaration of Independence, the role of the

Constitution and the Bill of Rights, then the country under his leadership would likely move back toward freedom.

But what if this leader just uses the anger of those who are already upset to gain personal power? What if he selects and generalizes about some group or race as being the problem within society? “It’s the Jews!”, “It’s the Mexicans!”, “It’s the Rich!”, “It’s the Politicians!”

What happens at this point?

The country would take another step toward the left with the help of the angry Right. It is another step away from freedom for all.

Could the rise of those who want freedom, actually result in another step toward enslavement?

You will see this more fully in the next government system which lies just to the left of Democratic Socialism.

Democratic Socialism is the demarcation between freedom and enslavement. This is the “middle” of the spectrum. Freedom and enslavement are in the balance.

Many modern Western democracies occupy this contested middle ground. Scandinavian countries, often praised as 'successful socialist' models, were functioning democracies with robust free-market economies through the mid-20th century. As they implemented increasingly expansive social programs and government control from the 1960s onward, they drifted left toward democratic socialism. They survive on the prosperity generated when they operated further right on the spectrum, but as socialist policies expand, these nations show signs of declining conditions, such as rising crime rates in previously safe cities, increasing ethnic tensions and social division, growing numbers dependent on government assistance, declining entrepreneurship, and young people emigrating to seek better opportunities elsewhere.

When you see "senseless violence" begin to erupt in a society because of injustices, real or propagated, when you see violence erupt between political sides, you are seeing the markings of a society on the tipping point between rational freedom and irrational force.

Below this point we enter what has been offered to you as "The Political Spectrum: Fascism vs. Communism."

Up to this point, the Right has tried to accept the Left's activities without violent protest, hoping good sense will win the day, only to be disappointed, over and over.

The Left has pushed its agenda little by little over decades, and even centuries, in an attempt not to create violent objection from the Right. But at this middle point, there is only one option left if it wants to reach its objectives and complete the enslavement of society.

At this stage, it is recognized by both sides that one or the other could resort to force.

The "Right", individual citizens, arm up while the Left weaponizes its agencies and works to remove the possibility of force from society. "Gun control" is the slogan, confiscation is the objective.

The Right is always the stronger force. But it does not mean they always win.

If the Left had the strength of the Right, it wouldn't use progressivism. This is why they work so long and patiently to degrade the morals, education, ethical and religious standards of a society.

How does a weaker Left overpower a stronger Right? It is called Bureaucracy.

Bureaucracy: excessive multiplication of, and concentration of power in, bureaus or administrators.

Bureaucratic abuse of individual rights is the first indication that a government is going out of control of the people and their elected representatives. By obtaining positions of "power" the Left can begin to "force" their will upon a free society.

If you have ever dealt with a government agency or individual who seemed to revel in their control over your activities or property, you have witnessed this Bureaucracy firsthand.

You often have recourse to a higher-up person who still understands they are there to serve the people and can act as a buffer to such abuse. But when enough of these weak, but determined people occupy positions of power in government, injustice becomes overwhelmingly heavy, and rights are trampled upon.

In our Republic, elected officials are empowered to write and enact laws. When this important duty is unconstitutionally delegated to administrators, they inevitably abuse this power if they fail to understand and support the concept of freedom and human rights.

What follows are mini "dictatorships", where agencies appear to have unlimited power over their domain and individual's rights become abused.

The most abusive American agencies are those which were created in violation of the Constitution. Some examples are:

-The Internal Revenue Service (IRS)

-National Security Agency (NSA)

-Environmental Protection Agency (EPA)

-U.S. Department of Education (DOE)

-U.S. Department of Energy (DOE)

These agencies, which have become a grave concern to American citizens and groups, are the result of lazy, ignorant and/or devious acts of Congress.

We can vote out the politicians who let us down. But we have little if any, recourse against agencies which write and enforce their own laws in violation of the U.S. Constitution.

Why are these agencies unconstitutional? The Constitution grants all legislative power to Congress (Article I, Section 1). When Congress delegates law-making authority to unelected bureaucrats, it violates this fundamental principle. These agencies create regulations with the force of law, without representation or accountability to the people.

The constitutional alternative is simple: Congress must write the laws, keep them few and clear, and limit agencies to purely administrative functions—carrying out laws, not creating them. Any agency that cannot justify its existence within the enumerated powers of Article I, Section 8 should be eliminated and its legitimate functions returned to the States or private sector.

When free people see their rights being infringed upon, their government causing injustices, the "Press" attacking their rights, their education system being corrupted, their politicians bowing to special interests rather than serving those who elected them, it is not hard to imagine what might follow.

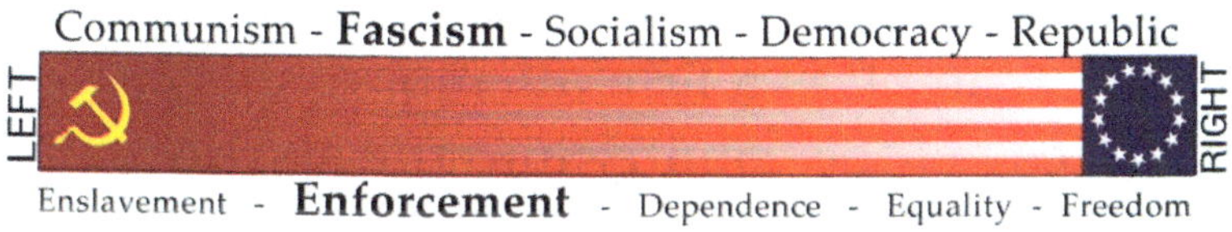

Fascism

Fascism: The term fascism was first used (by) the totalitarian right-wing nationalist regime of Mussolini in Italy (1922–43); the regimes of the Nazis in Germany and Franco in Spain were also forms of Fascism.

> Fascism tends to include a belief in the supremacy of one national or ethnic group, a contempt for democracy, an insistence on obedience to a powerful leader, and a strong demagogic* approach.

Fascism allows no political opposition (especially democracy, socialism or communism) and forcibly suppresses dissent. It rigidly controls most industrial and economic activities.

Fascism is the last-ditch effort of the populist Right to keep its country from sliding into communism. This is why the Communist and Fascist are such enemies.

The rise of Italian dictator, Benito Mussolini, was an effort to protect the country from socialism and communism.

"Solidarity" of *The State* occurs at this level of the spectrum. It is a firm attempt to prevent further decay of the country into the slavery of communism. It is a very angry and turbulent affair.

When a large portion of the society is convinced that their last remnant of freedom is at risk, they will accept the idea that this strong and fearless man is their last chance to save their country.

There is no allowance or tolerance for democratic, socialistic or communistic opposition. There is also no real freedom.

In 2012, the elections in Greece support this data. Facing the chaotic breakdown of Socialism, the Greek people voted in the Golden Dawn political party, which was considered a fascist nationalistic political system.

People around the world scratched their heads at this result. However, based on the data in this book, it was natural progression and completely predictable. These people were desperately trying to avoid the slide into communism and the complete ruin of their country.

Mussolini placed the highest value on the survival of *The State*. All else, including its citizens, were assigned value in relation to their support of *The State*.

> ***"The foundation of Fascism is the conception of the State, its character, its duty, and its aim. Fascism conceives of the State as an absolute, in comparison with which all individuals or groups are relative, only to be conceived of in their relation to the State."***

Here can be seen the decay of personal freedom when the State is all and the individual only a secondary consideration. So, no, there is no real freedom in this final mutation of a free society.

One can easily extrapolate the role of the press, education and religion in fascism. These would all be under the control of the dictator and aligned with the ideals of the State and thus explain the rise of State Religions in certain fascist States.

Religion becomes a tool to sanction the power of the State through the chosen religion. Any religion which falls for this false role, betraying its real purpose, will eventually lose the support of its congregation. (Financing from the State may substitute for the falling donations from its congregation.)

One can see many <u>similarities</u> between the far right (Republic) and this fascist band on the left. Though there are similarities, they are most certainly <u>not</u> the same.

In a republic, government serves the people. It takes action to protect individual rights and freedoms. In fascism, the people serve the State, and their freedoms are only as sanctioned by the State.

One might conceive that the Left took advantage of these similarities and placed Fascism to the extreme right on the political spectrum to confuse or to use as a “weapon”, a tactic, to demonize those on the right. They portray men who argue for freedom as people who want to lead society into the extremes of fascism.

But it may be more accurate to conclude that those who truly believe that communism is the best solution for man, cannot really conceive of the true nature of a republic: That government has the role of serving its citizens and freedom is the natural state of man.

This concept is as alien to such men as the concept of God is to an atheist. They reject it with all of their being.

Communists covertly attack the concept of The State. He tells the “workers” (or “Labor”) how they are being oppressed and should rise up against the State. And in the final bid for total equality, convinces a portion of the populace they will only have equality when THE PEOPLE forcefully take back power from THE STATE.

It is always a bloody revolution, this step from Fascism to Communism. Those who advocated such ideas as liberty, individual rights, and religious freedom, either flee the country or are slaughtered.

Despite the promises from communist activists, the power does not pass back to the people, but to a collective “People”, controlled by the Chairman of the Communist Party.

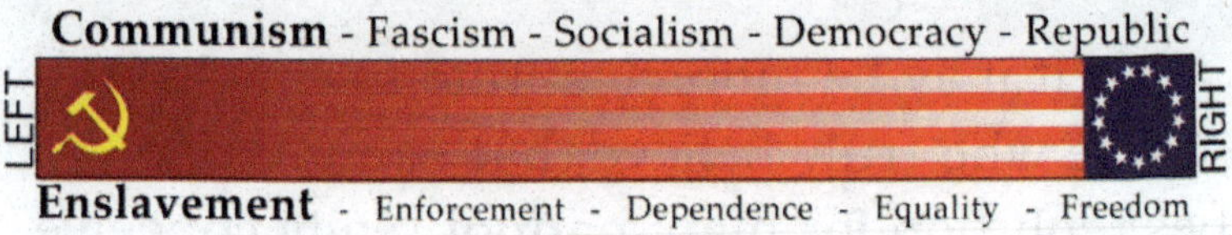

Communism

To the left of Fascism is the concept of a total breakdown and elimination of the State as an identity, and the eradication of private property.

Communism sells itself as “a worker’s paradise, where all are truly equal.” What underlies this promise is the concept that no one should be wealthier than anyone else. The solution to this “problem” is to make it illegal for anyone to own anything, while quelling any objections by stating that everyone owns everything. Objections solved!

Communism forwards the idea of no State and no country, as an ideal. They often refer to themselves as “internationalists” and strive for a “one world government”. The creation of the European Union is part of this effort (though there are other forces involved in this which you will see later.)

The communist principle of, *"from each according to his ability, to each according to his needs"* is enforced upon its people. Any motivation to excel, work hard or create new, more efficient ways to produce a product is squashed by the simple reason that no one really cares anymore. There is no reward for hard work or bright ideas so why work hard? Why dream?

When a hard-working person sees a comrade loafing, who is yet receiving the same benefits, his own level of production begins to drop.

He may even try to get the loafer to work harder. But his comrade asks, "Will I get more food?" It is a rhetorical question of course. And thus, overall production goes down and so does the standard of living and eventually everyone is equally miserable.

Study any communist controlled country and the misery is self-evident.

As illustrated by the spectrum's dichotomy, the individual's existence corresponds to the definition of a slave. He loses all control of his productivity and any reward he may reap from it. Nor is he free to leave.

He now works for "The People" and is paid back with what he "needs to survive". And when you look at any communist country, you will see that the meaning of "needs" is reduced to bare survival items, barely.

And thus, he is forced to become a criminal to actually survive. The black market becomes a secondary economic system of the country: An illegal "free market."

In the words of Stalin (Russian communist leader):

> ***"Democracy means equality. The great significance of labour's struggle for equality and of equality as a slogan will be clear if we correctly interpret it as meaning the abolition of classes.***
>
> ***"But democracy means only formal equality. And as soon as equality is achieved for all members of society in relation to ownership of the means of production, that is, equality of labor and wages, humanity will inevitably be confronted with the question of advancing farther, from formal equality to actual equality, i.e., to the operation of the rule 'from each according to his ability, to each according to his needs' ".***

Stalin assumed that people would see "equality" as an ideal condition through democracy and will then want even more, in the form of communism.

Communist propaganda operates on man's emotions. Obviously, there has always been a level of unrest and gullibility in man. Perhaps educated about the real political spectrum, this will not always be the case.

Through his winding theory of materialism, Marx accomplished his first objective: to eliminate God from man's existence and proposed that life sprung accidently and by chance, out of the evolution of random forces of matter.

Communism was formed on the notion that a supreme being does not exist. Its first basic "law" is that life came from matter, through numberless random mistakes and had no master divine plan or guidance.

It takes a very ignorant or blind eye to not at once shoot this theory to pieces. The best place to start is with the idea that life is an accidental, random act of matter. This would naturally eliminate the idea of "purpose" and thus a "plan".

But can anyone look at an ear and not state its purposc? Is there not a multitude of organs and coordinated systems within man which to each can be assigned an exact purpose? What would be the odds of each of these purposes randomly and accidentally coming together with no plan?

Great men seek to raise other men to new levels of freedom and personal responsibility, and they have a strong love for their fellow man. From their teachings are built ethical individuals and great societies and cultures.

Evil men seek to tear down societies and reduce man's desires for freedom. They strive to increase man's fears and use these to entrap him in insecurities and hate.

This is often done by spreading rumors and lies about men or groups of good will.

Their lies break down the trust and affinity between people and groups. So "sympathetic" are their words, so "caring" they appear, but with rumor, innuendo or authoritative utterances they wear down love or trust toward one another.

What happens when production dwindles so low that communism can no longer support itself and eventually implodes upon itself?

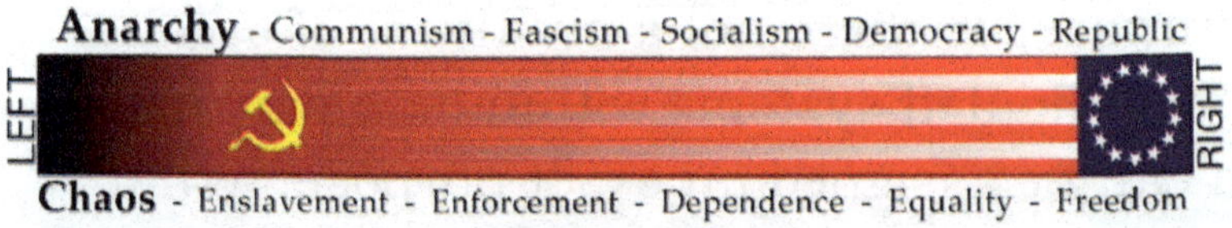

ANARCHY

There is a political condition (not a system) to the left of communism which has also been routinely placed on the far right; Anarchy.

There are two definitions of Anarchy in the dictionary. The first describes a condition brought about as a result of a collapse of an existing government.

Anarchy - Definition 1:

Political and social disorder due to the absence of governmental control.

In this condition, citizens begin to band into "organized cartels" in order to survive, such as was seen in the rise of the Russian mafia after the collapse of communism. This is a very unstable state of affairs and there are no guarantees of personal freedom or justice.

The second definition of Anarchy defines a state of social order maintained by the civil actions of the individual. Man would have to rise to a higher state of responsibility and ethical behavior to obtain such an ideal. But as it is a higher level of freedom, it certainly would fit to the right of a republic.

Anarchy - Definition 2:

A theory that regards the absence of all direct government as a political ideal, and which proposes the cooperative and voluntary association of the individuals and groups as the principal mode of organized society.

So, when a person declares himself an anarchist, it would be a good idea to look at his actions to see which side of the scale he is operating on.

If he is assisting in bringing order to the society and speaks of individual responsibility and freedom for all, you might call him a creative anarchist, though the term Libertarian may define him as well.

However, the anarchist you usually see or hear about is advocating violence and the downfall of whatever social order exists. Such people could be called destructive anarchists. They are quite easy to see, even if their faces are hidden by masks.

Chapter Nine

Ignorance – the Slave Master's Most Powerful Weapon

What You Don't Know Can Hurt You

A major difference between fascism and communism is their method of advancement.

Fascism is outright confrontational. There is little if anything hidden about its agenda. What you see is what you get. Disagree and you find someone on your doorstep, very publicly removing you from the environment, making an obvious example to others who would disagree. This is known as a Police State.

Communism, however, is quite secretive from beginning to end, always keeping its actual intentions hidden, always putting on a show.

What you hear about is usually intended to distract, placate or divert attention. What you see is the opposite of what you will get. Disagree and you likely die or disappear quietly in the night.

Covert operations are the mainstay of communism. The whole Cold War mentality was covert actions fighting covert actions. This force is known as the Secret Police.

There is no room or need for "secret police" or "covert actions" in a republic. Why would there be if this data were understood and used?

What you don't know can hurt you.

In communism, "mental health" is a tool used to cure people of their obsession to objecting to being slaves.

Electric and chemical shock are tools used to quiet dissidents. Strong psychotropic drugs are used to reduce free will and in some cases the will to live.

This same methodology has infiltrated Western mental health systems. Rather than addressing root causes of distress, the focus has shifted to chemical control through prescription drugs. The results speak for themselves: rising suicide rates despite widespread medication, and a disturbing pattern of mass violence linked to psychiatric drugs.

According to Department of Veterans Affairs data, an average of twenty veterans per day committed suicide following the Iraq War—despite (or perhaps because of) widespread prescription of psychotropic medications. This raises serious questions about whether these treatments heal or simply suppress the individual's will to resist their circumstances.

Communism is not a worker's paradise, but a free man's nightmare. It is in fact very difficult for individuals in a free society to actually confront that such a group of people exist or should be taken seriously.

Anyone who can and does vocally confront what the left is doing is likely to be labeled paranoid or mentally ill. The use of "Mental Therapy" quiets such talk.

What you don't know will hurt you

The very inability and unwillingness to face and observe the intentions and objectives of the communist mind is the very basis of any success it has.

As detestable as it may be, a free society should not only be educated in its own culture but in the intentions and objectives of communism and tyranny.

As mentioned earlier, the goal of this book was to build an understanding of each political system and their relationships with each other and their citizens. Here also is added another goal, to provide an understanding of the tools the far Left use relentlessly to tear the fabric of a free society.

What you know may help you

The following are a few snippets of communist doctrine. One should read the words of communist leaders and understand that these are the actual methods being used to enslave populations, even today.

In the words of Vladimir Lenin, (Article: What Is to Be Done? BURNING QUESTIONS OF OUR MOVEMENT.)

> **"Attention must be devoted principally, *to raising* the workers to the level of revolutionaries; it is not at all our task *to descend* to the level of the 'working masses'."**

Workers are first united into unions, and they become dependent on their unions. Union members receive personal benefits and enhanced survival for themselves and their family. They may occasionally, individually, question the motives of its organizers, but any threat to the union becomes a threat to the individual, and thus union members can be made to act violently to protect the survival of their group and thus themselves, their personal survival being so entwined.

You may also have noticed in the above quote, that communist leaders do not look at themselves as equal to the worker. An obvious departure from the equality they so eloquently preach.

What you know will help you

The role of the Press in bringing about a communist takeover is made very clear in an article written by J. V. Stalin on May 6, 1923, THE PRESS AS A COLLECTIVE ORGANIZER.

> ***"The role of a newspaper is not limited, however, merely to the spreading of ideas, merely to political education and attracting political allies. A newspaper is not only a collective propagandist and a collective agitator; it is also a collective organizer....***
>
> ***"This network of agents*** (in the media) ***will form the skeleton of precisely the organization we need, namely, one that is sufficiently large to embrace the whole country; sufficiently wide and many-sided to affect a strict and detailed division of labour; sufficiently tried and tempered to be able unswervingly to carry on its own work under all***

circumstances, at all 'turns,' and in all contingencies; sufficiently flexible to be able to avoid open battle against an enemy of overwhelming strength when he has concentrated all his forces at one spot; and yet able to take advantage of the unwieldiness of this enemy and to attack him when and where least expected."

Compare the use of the Press by the Left to the role of the Press on the Right. Where the Press on the Right is a force for freedom, the role of the Press on the Left is used for the covert downfall and enslavement of a nation.

A study of the above quote enlightens one on the use of the Press by communist agents spread throughout the media world.

The very protections and freedoms that our society provides for a free Press, opens itself to the covert use of its press in spreading communist-propaganda, agitation and organizing.

The communist party understands that a "communist newspaper" would be completely ineffective, because its message would be ignored by a free people. Covert, hidden, and secretive use of the Press are the only effective means to accomplish their purpose.

You may have become aware that the "mainstream" media does not uncover abuses to the Constitution, unless it applies specifically to Freedom of the Press! In other words, an attempt to stop them from their mission to forward their message and propaganda.

It has become clear that the Press has been thwarted from its role of watchdog.

The bastions of free press which still remain are attacked as extreme right-wing activists. Well, in fact, they are much further to the right than the left even understands.

Not only does the free press have the job of reporting on an overreaching government, it also has the obligation, and must report on, and clean up the unethical activities within the Press itself. The Press is the only watch dog of the press that can really exist.

This self-oversite is easier than it may seem. All one has to do is uncover the truth where it is perverted or covered up. Truth always trumps a lie. And when lies are exposed, trust is forfeited by those spreading the lie.

Examples of how the Press has become a collective propagandist, agitator and organizer can be seen in the way they attacked and demonized the Tea Party's attempt to move our government back under the Constitution. Apparently, according to these agitators, it is scandalous for citizens to take actions to hold government to the Constitution.

But these same agitators and organizers popularized “Occupy Wall Street” gatherings, which represented discontent with our political and economic system, support of class warfare and anarchy.

If you understand the Left’s system of destroying a society, you easily see what they are doing and what they intend. When you know this, their methods become much less effective.

What you know might save you.

Chapter Ten

Enemies of Freedom

Part I

Fascism

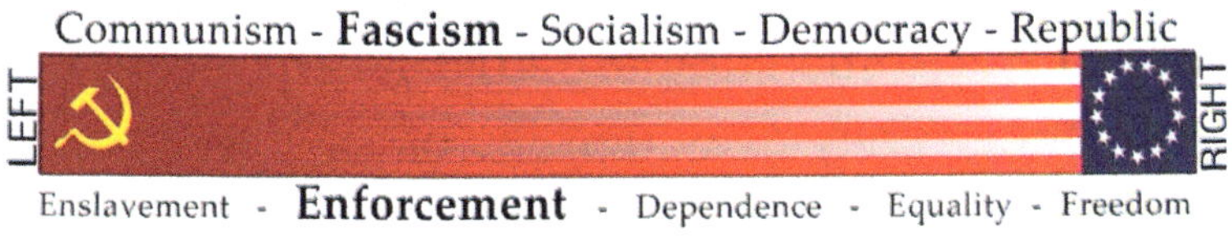

It has been said that the difference between insanity and sanity has an exact point. Does the person's or group's action result in creation or destruction? We're not talking about institutional insanity here. We're talking about intentions and actions of a person and their effects on those around them.

When you look at the political spectrum, you could place 'destruction' on the left, and 'construction' on the right. There are many descriptive words that fit on the extreme ends of this dichotomy, including 'sanity' and 'insanity'. All that we consider good in man, you would find on the right. All that we consider evil in man, you will find, in plenty, on the left.

But there are no absolutes. Even in the "most evil man", one can find some good and something to love. In the most virtuous man, one could still find some reason to distrust. Man is a fragile being prone to various impulses, good and bad.

The far Left, Communism and Fascism, are enemies of freedom. They are enemies of independence. They are enemies of all that one would strive to achieve on the side of Freedom.

Fascism, though posing as a savior of freedom, is yet an enemy because it uses the last hopes and dreams of freedom and drowns them in oppressive government force and control.

Leaders of both fascism and communism despise liberty and freedom. They have no trust in, or love for their fellow man or Providence, but only cling to their twisted ideologies.

Benito Mussolini, the dictator of Italy in the early part of the 20th century, assisted in the destruction of Europe and ultimately his own country. What were his views? What mentality existed? What did he love? What did he hate? Where was his anger directed? Let's look at these quotes for the answers.

Benito Mussolini Quotes:

Fascism on Freedom:

"We have buried the putrid corpse of liberty."

Fascism on Religion:

"The history of saints is mainly the history of insane people."

"Fascism is a religion. The twentieth century will be known in history as the century of Fascism."

"Fascism is a religious concept."

Fascism on Education:

"It is the State which educates its citizens in civic virtue, gives them a consciousness of their mission and welds them into unity."

"Fascist education is moral, physical, social, and military: it aims to create a complete and harmoniously developed human, a fascist one according to our views."

Fascism on communism:

> ***"State <u>ownership</u>! It leads only to absurd and monstrous conclusions; state ownership means state monopoly, concentrated in the hands of one party and its adherents, and that state brings only ruin and bankruptcy to all."***

You can see here, in the words of Mussolini, why communists despise and fear fascism. It is also why they call anyone who opposes them a fascist.

Nazism (Nationalism)

Adolf Hitler sacked most of Europe via Germany in World War II. Germany was all but destroyed as a result of his leftist mentality and actions.

As a result, he left half of his people (East Germany) under the control of the Russian communist and their brutal enslavement.

Hitler had these views.

Hitler's quotes:

On Truth and his view of his Fellow Man:

"It is not truth that matters, but victory."

"What luck for rulers that men do not think."

"But the most brilliant propagandist technique will yield no success unless one fundamental principle is borne in mind constantly and with unflagging attention. It must confine itself to a few points and repeat them over and over. Here, as so often in this world, persistence is the first and most important requirement for success."

"The great masses of the people will more easily fall victims to a big lie than to a small one."

"If you tell a big enough lie and tell it frequently enough, it will be believed."

"By the skillful and sustained use of propaganda, one can make a people see even heaven as hell or an extremely wretched life as paradise."

"The victor will never be asked if he told the truth."

"The receptivity of the masses is very limited, their intelligence is small, but their power of forgetting is enormous. In consequence of these facts, all effective propaganda must be limited to a very few points and must harp on these in slogans until the last member of the public understands what you want him to understand by your slogan."

Hitler on Education:

"The man, who has no sense of history, is like a man who has no ears or eyes."

"He alone, who owns the youth, gains the future."

"I begin with the young. We older ones are used up but my magnificent youngsters! Are there finer ones anywhere in the world? Look at all these men and boys! What material! With you and I, we can make a new world."

Hitler on Commerce:

"Industry, technology, and commerce can thrive only as long as an idealistic national community offers the necessary preconditions. And these do not lie in material egoism, but in a spirit of sacrifice and joyful renunciation."

Hitler on America:

"I don't see much future for the Americans ... it's a decayed country. And they have their racial problem, and the problem of social inequalities ... my feelings against Americanism are feelings of hatred and deep repugnance ... everything about the behavior of American society reveals that it's half Judaised, and the other half negrified. How can one expect a State

like that to hold together?"

Hitler on his own demise:

> *"When people attempt to rebel against the iron logic of Nature, they come into conflict with the very same principles to which they owe their existence as human beings. Their actions against Nature must lead to their own downfall."*

Notice that fascism is very straightforward about its views, hates and anger. There really is nothing hidden in their motives. If you look at the various Fascist/Nazi followers around the world, they will tell you what they believe and who they are against. They will tell you who they hate.

Within a free society, even people of this mentality can live, because laws exist to thwart their evil impulses, until perhaps they can be educated out of them. Or they break the laws and end up secluded from society.

It would be nice if we could end this book here. Fascists are such easy targets. They are so visible. Their hate and anger are bullseyes they pin on their own foreheads.

But if the next two chapters were to be ignored, any efforts to renew freedom in America or any free society would fail. If you are willing to look, you will know what follows is true. It may be difficult to look at, but you have everything to gain if you do. The alternative is the loss of your freedom if you do not.

If reading the next chapters begins to become unreal to you, or if it raises hatred, anger or fear, simply step back for a moment, examine your love for freedom, and with that, your ability to tolerate the next man's rights and freedoms.

Increase your determination to act and support those who work for your freedoms. If you can do this, you will see how love for your fellow man, (even your enemies) will get you through and allow you to be free.

I only point this out, because hate, fear and anger can only draw you down into fascist solutions.

No matter how good the intentions. Good people can act very badly when they buy into the lies of fascist and communist propaganda.

Chapter Eleven

Enemies of Freedom

Part II

Communism

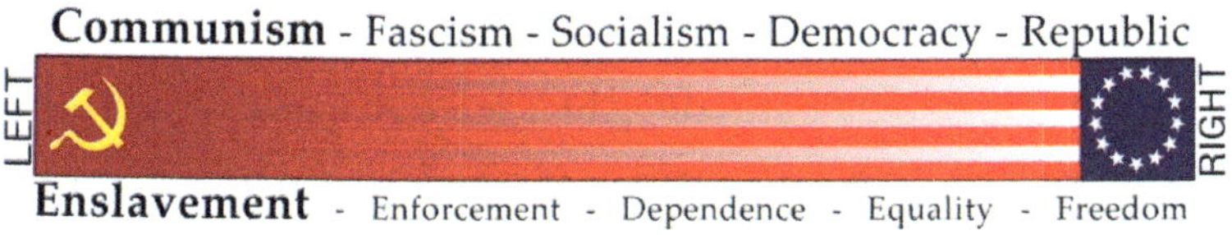

Communism is a major threat and enemy to a Free Society. Why?

Communism is a threat, only because their actions are hidden, kept secret and ardently denied.

They ally themselves with and infiltrate many unsuspecting groups, who unknowingly give their hidden ideas voice and action. They keep their intentions hidden and deny vehemently any accusations made toward them.

Sound like paranoia? Unfortunately, there's nothing delusional about this book. The only delusion might be that enough Americans will wake up before the Left drags us all into a violent revolution and possibly a tyranny that could threaten not just the U.S., but the rest of the world.

The far left are in fact cowards; determined, nonetheless. As with the "jealous" cowardly villain in any Hollywood movie, they slip and slide around their victims telling comforting lies here, planting deceit there.

Direct conflict is avoided at all costs. They gain control of the "working class" through their propaganda to bring down a society. They infiltrate worker unions. They make workers dependent and when ready for revolt, create fear that the worker's personal survival is threatened and thus the uprising of "the worker".

A great example of the difference between the far left and far right would be Germany after WWII. While everyone else was celebrating the end of the war and beginning to work on the reconstruction plans of Europe, the Russian communists, who had been "allies" of the West during the war, did what they possibly had been planning all along; they moved in on the collapsed fascist state of Germany and other east European countries and put them under the yoke of communism.

Perhaps they had planned to grab more of Europe after the war. If America had not been there, Europe might look very different today. What kind of people would do that? Only people who hate liberty and care nothing for the welfare of their fellow man.

Perhaps America stood between them and their ambitions. Perhaps that's why America became the next target on their agenda. They hadn't expected a free society to step in and help win the war.

Communism is a political party in our country. It is actually quite small in numbers relative to the overall population.

They covertly aligned themselves with many political allies and activist groups and have slowly persuaded these groups into certain actions which began the decay of society.

They work within the system, creating regulations that cripple companies, groups and individuals. Most of the people you see on these front lines are themselves not communists; they are too brave and too direct. But they are being orchestrated by the communists in the background, who is not in the public eye.

You see this in Hollywood all the time. Artists are not really communists, but are easily persuaded by leftist propaganda, perhaps by those who hold the purse strings of their acting careers.

If it were not so serious, it would be laughable to point out that no one is actually threatening, attacking or trying to harm the communist. They really have no reason to be afraid. It is their own distorted view of life, mankind and their impulse to destroy (which is as real and powerful to them as the impulse you may feel toward freedom) which drives them.

The difference is, where the communist has nothing to be afraid of from freedom-loving people, the same cannot be said for those who are trying to live a life under freedom and human rights.

The reasons for a free nation's difficulties, wars and downfall can all be seen, throughout history, to be the overt or covert attacks on freedom, thus requiring a defense against slavery and tyranny, whether real or artificially created.

For a free nation, the solution to communism is very simple, almost too simple to believe. The solution is to understand communism, to understand how they operate. You do not have to outlaw them. They could and would simply change their name as they always do.

It is their methods that stand out, not their name. All one has to do is educate the citizens, *all* citizens, especially political students, about philosophy, tactics and methods of communism no matter how repulsive that may seem.

The keepers of freedom should know the enemies of freedom; otherwise, freedom falls victim.

Like termites eating the structure of a home, going unnoticed for years, with only small signs of decay, if ignored, no matter how many coats of paint are applied to hide the decay, the whole structure grows weak and during a storm when strength is needed most, the structure comes down.

When studying the works of communism, it must be pointed out again and again that they are fighting the ogre known as The State. That's what they see. That's what they fight.

Communism must be looked at from their viewpoint to be understandable. They cannot see past the "group" to see the individual. They only see people as "masses", "classes" or the collective "People".

They can no more conceive of a free society being desirable than George Washington could have envisioned the subjugation of those who populated the colonies after the Revolutionary War. He was asked to be King. He refused.

As for communism taking down a republic, it is first necessary for them to bring it down to a level of fascism before it can affect its final blow. A republic could never fall from the heights of liberty directly to the depths of communism. A free society is too strong and free. It has to be brought down step by step over a long period of time... centuries. Cultures change slowly. It takes a long time to crush any hope of freedom in people, which must occur before communism can take hold.

During final research, an article was discovered which contained a portion of the book, **The Naked Communist,** by W. Cleon Skousen.

If all the data above were not enough to make it important to publish this book, a sudden look at fifty years of covert communist aggression against the American people made it vital.

The Naked Communist was written in 1958. The goals of the communist party were laid bare. It became a best seller in the U.S. in the early 1960s. But men went back to work, apparently feeling that the government would now do its job and protect them since all was now exposed.

After all, this list of communist objectives for America had even been read on the floor of the House of Representatives on January 10th 1963 by a Florida congressman and made public record.

But nothing effective happened. It is certain that some freedom loving men kept watch and kept pointing out the warning signs. They were likely called fanatics and insane. People did not want to hear.

Now that 50 years have passed, it becomes sadly apparent that the author reported the truth and nothing effective was done by America, its people or its government leaders.

So, while America was whistling past the graveyard, communists and their financial supporters have been hard at work. You will see this in the final portion of this chapter.

The phrase “hindsight is 20/20 vision” is very appropriate here. We have an opportunity to put on rearview mirrors and look back over a period of more than 50 years from when this data was revealed, something that could not have been done in early 1960 when the book was released.

It is recommended to not just read the following list through. Do your own online research on each point of the list, especially if an objective on this list means nothing to you. Research it like your freedom depends on it.

(Notes in brackets {} were added for clarification only.)

[From "The Naked Communist," by Cleon Skousen]
1958: CURRENT COMMUNIST GOALS

1. U.S. acceptance of coexistence {with communist Russia} as the only alternative to atomic war.

2. U.S. willingness to capitulate* in preference to engaging in atomic war.

3. Develop the illusion that total disarmament [by] the United States would be a demonstration of moral strength.

4. Permit free trade between all nations regardless of Communist affiliation and regardless of whether or not items could be used for war.

5. Extension of long-term loans to Russia and Soviet satellites {Soviet Controlled States}.

6. Provide American aid to all nations regardless of Communist domination.

7. Grant recognition of Red China. Admission of Red China to the U.N.

8. Set up East and West Germany as separate states in spite of Khrushchev's promise in 1955 to settle the

German question by free elections under supervision of the U.N.

9. Prolong the conferences to ban atomic tests because the United States has agreed to suspend tests as long as negotiations are in progress.

10. Allow all Soviet satellites individual representation in the U.N.

11. Promote the U.N. as the only hope for mankind. If its charter is rewritten, demand that it be set up as a one-world government with its own independent armed forces. (Some Communist leaders believe the world can be taken over as easily by the U.N. as by Moscow. Sometimes these two centers compete with each other as they are now doing in the Congo.)

12. Resist any attempt to outlaw the Communist Party.

13. Do away with all loyalty oaths. (Such as the pledge of allegiance)

14. Continue giving Russia access to the U.S. Patent Office.

15. Capture one or both of the political parties in the United States.

16. Use technical decisions of the courts to weaken basic American institutions by claiming their activities violate civil rights.

17. Get control of the schools. Use them as transmission belts for socialism and current Communist propaganda. Soften the curriculum. Get

control of teachers' associations. Put the party line in textbooks.

18. Gain control of all student newspapers.

19. Use student riots to foment public protests against programs or organizations which are under Communist attack. (Such as constructive capitalism and the free-market systems)

20. Infiltrate the press. Get control of book-review assignments, editorial writing, and policy making positions.

21. Gain control of key positions in radio, TV, and motion pictures.

22. Continue discrediting American culture by degrading all forms of artistic expression. An American Communist cell was told to "eliminate all good sculpture from parks and buildings, substitute shapeless, awkward and meaningless forms."

23. Control art critics and directors of art museums. "Our plan is to promote ugliness, repulsive, meaningless art."

24. Eliminate all laws governing obscenity by calling them "censorship" and a violation of free speech and free press.

25. Break down cultural standards of morality by promoting pornography and obscenity in books, magazines, motion pictures, radio, and TV.

26. Present homosexuality, degeneracy and promiscuity as "normal, natural, healthy."

27. Infiltrate the churches and replace revealed religion* with "social" religion*. Discredit the Bible and emphasize the need for intellectual maturity which does not need a "religious crutch."

28. Eliminate prayer or any phase of religious expression in the schools on the ground that it violates the principle of "separation of church and state."

29. Discredit the American Constitution by calling it inadequate, old-fashioned, out of step with modern needs, a hindrance to cooperation between nations on a worldwide basis.

30. Discredit the American Founding Fathers. Present them as selfish aristocrats who had no concern for the "common man."

31. Belittle all forms of American culture and discourage the teaching of American history on the ground that it was only a minor part of the "big picture." Give more emphasis to Russian history since the Communists took over.

32. Support any socialist movement to give centralized control over any part of the culture: education, social agencies, welfare programs, mental health clinics, etc.

33. Eliminate all laws or procedures which interfere with the operation of the Communist apparatus.

34. Eliminate the House Committee on Un-American Activities.

35. Discredit and eventually dismantle the FBI.

36. Infiltrate and gain control of more unions.

37. Infiltrate and gain control of big business.

38. Transfer some of the powers of arrest from the police to social agencies. Treat all behavioral problems as psychiatric disorders which no one but psychiatrists can understand [or treat].

39. Dominate the psychiatric profession and use mental health laws as a means of gaining coercive control over those who oppose Communist goals.

40. Discredit the family as an institution. Encourage promiscuity and easy divorce.

41. Emphasize the need to raise children away from the negative influence of parents. Attribute prejudices, mental blocks and retarding of children to suppressive influence of parents.

42. Create the impression that violence and insurrection are legitimate aspects of the American tradition; that students and special-interest groups should rise up and use ["] united force ["] to solve economic, political or social problems.

43. Overthrow all colonial governments before native populations are ready for self-government.

44. Internationalize the Panama Canal.

45. Repeal the Connally Reservation so the United States cannot prevent the World Court from seizing jurisdiction [over domestic problems. Give the World Court jurisdiction] over nations and individuals alike.

EDITORIAL NOTE: Of the 45 goals listed above from 1958, a disturbing number have been achieved or are in advanced stages of implementation:

FULLY ACHIEVED: Goals 7, 11, 13, 14, 15, 16, 17, 18, 19, 20, 21, 24, 25, 26, 27, 28, 29, 32, 34, 36, 40, 41, 44

SUBSTANTIALLY ACHIEVED: Goals 1, 3, 4, 6, 12, 22, 23, 30, 31, 33, 35, 37, 38, 39, 42, 43, 45

IN PROGRESS: Goals 2, 5, 8, 9, 10

The reader is encouraged to research each goal independently to verify these assessments. What seemed like alarmist predictions in 1958 can now be evaluated against sixty-seven years of evidence.

It might be a good idea for *THE NAKED COMMUNIST*, as well as its companion book, *THE NAKED CAPITALIST*, to become bestsellers again.

What was perhaps a list of possibilities and seemingly unlikely probabilities when written in 1958, can now be seen as actualities.

Communism is a problem for a free society, and its motives and actions must be understood to maintain or reduce the negative effects it causes.

The next chapter saves the worst for last.

The individuals that follow are in fact in a position to affect enormous positive changes in society and instead have only the conquest of nations, power and personal greed as their motives. Perhaps it is a game of the rich and idle to dream of planetary conquest but to never really look at those who inhabit the world.

Imagine the self-importance of people who are willing to cause millions to die in order to implement their selfish plans.

One can only wonder what justifications they tell themselves and each other for what they do to tear down societies and destroy millions of lives, families, groups and nations.

Chapter Twelve

Enemies of Freedom

Part III

Capitalists Behind the Curtain,

The Central Bank Façade

As our society spirals toward socialism, it has been seen that a few prominent capitalists publicly promote and support implementation of socialistic policies while other capitalists denounce them.

Remember, capitalism as defined in this book, cannot stand on its own as an economic system. It cannot exist without the Free Market. It produces nothing tangible from which to make a profit. It depends on production of a privately-owned business to obtain a profit for money invested.

It is vitally important to understand the difference between Free-Market economics and Capitalism. People working in the free market are producing and selling products.

A person becomes a capitalist when he has sufficient wealth to invest in another person's production with the intention of receiving a share of the profit.

In socialism, the means of production begins to shift from private ownership to government ownership. People who worked for themselves or an employer are now producing for the government. Government now has a means of producing tangible products that can be sold and thus government has entered the "free market".

Capitalists, theoretically, could invest their wealth in government efforts to take over certain private sector businesses, such as utilities, communications, transportation, healthcare, etc. All "profits" would now belong to those in government, and a share would come back to the capitalist who financed the activity. It is a feasible theory.

Taken to an extreme, capitalists could invest in political, social and propaganda activities which will move public acceptance toward government takeover of more and more privately-owned businesses, with the end-goal of communism (complete ownership of all production) and make it seem acceptable to the public.

When full government takeover of all means of production occurs, the investing capitalists would see huge returns on their investment. With communism in place, production of the entire country becomes the basis of their investment return, and the wealth of these capitalists would greatly multiply.

Could a group of capitalists really do this? The answer is disturbingly “Yes”. They already have done it and are doing it to America:

> **Central Bank:** a national bank that provides financial and banking services for its country’s government and commercial banking system, as well as implementing the government’s monetary policy and issuing currency.

The above definition sounds legitimate and harmless. Notably missing from it, however, intentionally, is the important fact that all central banks are privately owned corporations. They are in fact capitalist enterprises which finance government activities for a huge profit.

What are these privately-owned central banks?

- Bank of England, (United Kingdom, 1694).

- The Federal Reserve (USA, Dec. 1913) and,

- All Central Banks in almost every country around the world.

These are not commercial banks. They are not government controlled financial institutions, though they usually appear to be.

They are associated and coordinated private ventures which fund and economically control governments and commercial banking systems around the world.

Central Banks loan "money" to both governments and commercial banks. You might ask where they get all of their money to loan. They seem to have unlimited wealth. The answer is simple. They create it from nothing.

Here's how it works: The Federal Reserve (and other central banks) have the legal authority to create currency. When the U.S. government needs money, the Treasury issues bonds—essentially IOUs promising to repay with interest. The Federal Reserve purchases these bonds by creating new money, either as physical currency or, more commonly today, as digital entries in bank accounts. This money didn't exist before—it was simply created by the stroke of a pen or keyboard.

The government now "owes" this newly created money back to the Federal Reserve, plus interest. To pay this debt, taxes must be collected from citizens. Thus, these private capitalists profit continuously from money they created at no cost, while citizens work to pay the interest through taxation.

This is fundamentally different from honest banking, where a bank loans based on the money it has from depositors. Central banks loan money they simply manufacture, giving them virtually unlimited power over governments and economies.

As mentioned earlier, profit ALWAYS depends on production. There is never profit without something produced and sold.

Government in a free society is not there to produce products which can be sold for a profit. So, if government is borrowing money from these private investors, (rather than collecting taxes or tariffs to cover its expenses) the first question one should ask is, “Why?” and the second is, “How is the ‘loan’ going to be paid back?”

Just prior to the implementation of the Federal Reserve, in December 1913, Congress established a collection system to take a share of each person's profit in the U.S., the Internal Revenue Service (IRS). What were they going to collect?

Income taxes in the United States became law in February 1913 with ratification of the 16th Amendment of the Constitution. This law provided the collection system necessary to pay back the loans received from the Federal Reserve.

The Income Tax law essentially gave the government the power to take a share of the profit produced through each and every individual's production. This power was forbidden in the Constitution.

The private capitalist now had in place the means to obtain a share of the profit from each and every working person in the United States.

The more government "borrows" from the Federal Reserve; the higher taxes must be raised to pay the interest on the "loan". Our government does not pay down the debt; it only pays the interest. Thus, the government's debt continues to climb, and the Federal Reserve has a never-ending flow of "profit" taken from the production of the American people.

Now you can see why certain wealthy capitalists support higher taxes. They are invested in government and become wealthier when taxes are increased.

Free-market capitalists fight higher taxes and regulations because it reduces a company's profit. Taxes and regulation reduce profits and lower returns on investments.

And thus, one can differentiate between the free-market capitalist and the government-controlling capitalist. It is best to know who the real enemies of freedom are, so that innocent people are not unjustly targeted.

Capitalism that assists to increase production might be called "constructive capitalism".

Capitalism, which funds and backs government activities, will always be destructive to your freedoms and rights.

When the government falls under the control of a central bank, that government begins to go out of control of its citizens.

As a citizen, you begin to lose control of your freedom, your production and your personal wealth. More and more of what you work for goes to these privately funded central banks via taxes collected by the very government which is supposed to protect your freedom and right to ownership.

This is a very dangerous situation for America or any free society.

Because current laws establish and protects these secret private capitalist activities, the only barriers they have in moving our government fully into communism are free-enterprises and you, the uppity American citizen, who insists on reducing government size and debt and maintaining a government by and for the people.

Those who would ridicule you for speaking out against too much government regulation, spending and growth are being financed to protect the investment of the central banks; of that you can be certain, directly or indirectly.

A society cannot remain free when a few have secretly usurped the powers of the individual. Government by and for the people has become government by and for the private bankers, who control and regulate government and economics.

Chapter Thirteen

The United States of America

A Republic in Trouble from its Beginning

When we envision a republic, there is an ideal which one may imagine and then there are the realities of life. A republic is not something one simply announces and then miraculously comes into being. It is something that has to be actively worked toward, every day, by at least some portion of society.

America, despite the ideal scene alluded to in its constitution, had major discrepancies already existing within its borders. Freeing men, women and children from slavery was heavily debated during the Continental Congress but not resolved. A whole society of Native Americans existed but their existence and rights were not resolved, resulting in injustices and the destruction of their cultures.

Why has the United States of America risen to such greatness? Some will say it is because of capitalism. Some will say it is because of blind ambition and greed. It is really neither of these.

Its greatness is the result of just one thing. America is great because of its love for freedom and human rights, period.

The more freedom is extended to all, the greater America becomes. All these other areas are successful because of the freedoms inherent in the formation of our country.

Our founding fathers did something very unusual in history. For the love and protection of freedom, they considered everything imaginable to ensure freedom for centuries to come in formulating our Constitution.

The Revolutionary War was fought for freedom from tyranny. It was fought for freedom. It was fought for the love of the concept of freedom and the envisioned rights that all men should be free.

What about the Civil War?

Some may say it was not fought to free the slaves. But when you look at the devastation to both North and South, was there any other result of any value which came from it?

The South had carried a terrible burden in its inequity to the slave. The Plantation Holders wanted their own freedom but refused it to fellow human beings. You cannot have it both ways.

Perhaps they brought ruin upon themselves. But the result of the war is that it brought freedom to more people.

The injustices committed against Native Americans represent another failure to uphold the Republic's founding principles. Treaties were made and broken. Lands were seized. Cultures were systematically destroyed through forced relocation and re-education programs. Native Americans were not granted citizenship until 1924, and many were denied voting rights until the 1960s.

Like slavery, these violations of human rights could not stand in a true republic. The path forward requires acknowledging these injustices occurred, honoring treaty obligations, and ensuring Native Americans enjoy the same rights and freedoms as all citizens. A republic based on human rights cannot exclude any group and remain true to its principles.

While the American Republic was ideal for those it served, inequities continued to exist which eventually had to be reconciled through civil protests. Those who sought to bring more rights and freedoms to minorities were the original liberals. They continued to push the idea of freedom for all.

Eventually the liberals fell victim to propaganda and infiltration from the far left and although their stated intentions always seemed good, their actions began to move the country toward the left.

What had been a force for freedom was manipulated into becoming "frontline soldiers" for the hidden objectives of communism and the downfall of America.

The conservatives began to fight the downward spiral of the Republic into democracy and now toward socialism, losing ground year by year.

The Republican Party itself fell victim to infiltration by the left. When a strong stance is required by the party to preserve freedom, those under the influence of the left, cast their votes against freedom. These politicians have become known as RINOs. (Republican In Name Only)

The majority of African Americans, having been freed from slavery (a condition found to the farthest left of the spectrum), did not possess the wherewithal, education or adaptability to raise themselves up to the level of the culture that existed around them.

Their freedom was declared, but their pain from slavery, loss of family and dignity was very deep. Without education and inclusion into society, there was little hope of a fast recovery from their oppressive condition.

The majority of African Americans remained uneducated, dependent and impoverished (a slightly higher condition than slavery on the spectrum). As a group, they have slowly found their faith, dignity and self-respect.

The Left can be seen courting their votes with promises but does little if anything to actually raise them up.

Despite and because of injustice after injustice and not being afforded the same rights as other men, the African American stood up and demanded his right to be part of the culture—to have his right to vote.

They crawled and clawed their way toward the right of the spectrum. Today, an increasing, if still small number, are participating in society and enjoying its freedoms. But the inequities continue.

Many African Americans see white people as their oppressors; to some, as enemies. It is not true. His only enemy is the hate and anger he holds onto, and which gets fomented by the left.

"I Have a Dream" invokes the love of man, not just for the man of color, but for all men. Martin Luther King, Jr. died for that dream of freedom like so many before him.

He believed in the dream of the Republic, freedom for all men. He raised the pride, hopes and dreams of the African American population and he also opened the eyes of a very large number of white people who had been walking through life with them closed to the injustices.

Love, not hate, is the only way that people can be raised to the level of a republic. The teachings of love by Buddha, Christ and Muhammad brought a civilizing influence on both East and West. But when religious beliefs are used to enslave and punish, or attack those with other religious beliefs, man once again sinks into a dark age.

As religions around the world are attacked or are used to oppress, man once again moves toward another dark age where his natural rights and urge toward freedom is being smothered.

Religions have a common purpose, and each should be respected. Where you see distrust and fear between religions, know that you are seeing the result of leftist propaganda quietly behind the scenes, creating hate.

It is vital to educate ALL American citizens on the fundamentals of our republic, the inherent rights of all men, and to move toward the actual practice of the principle: *We hold these truths to be self-evident, that all men are created equal, that they are endowed by their Creator with certain unalienable Rights, that among these are Life, Liberty and the pursuit of Happiness.*

These fundamentals are a major part of resolving the decay of America. What made America great is still capable of increasing that greatness.

Freedom loving people tend to trust other people until they show that they are untrustworthy. They often give many chances to others. But eventually, they may just shun those who hate and are anti-social.

Laws become necessary to handle the non-producer (the criminal), as they are rarely quiet or inactive. Police forces are formed to handle them, so the average citizen does not have to. Thus, the citizens grow weak in their ability to look at those who would do them harm.

Let the police handle it. Let the government handle it. Let the city council handle it. But what if the groups created to handle these problems were taken over by the very people they were supposed to protect the citizens from?

What happens when a police force becomes corrupt? Injustice.

What happens when government becomes corrupt? Loss of freedom.

The matter of who is qualified to vote in the Republic is an important subject. A republic is not a democracy. An important policy is to provide equality for all men under the law.

The Bill of Rights and The Constitution apply to every citizen.

The privilege to vote must be earned. Not being able to cast a vote does not limit the freedoms and rights of people in a republic. In fact, it may protect their rights.

The idea that the right to vote is the most important right a person has is just leftist propaganda, striving to decline a republic into democracy.

The main concern in determining the electorate (those who have a right to vote) is their honesty and understanding of the Constitution, not their education or how much they own.

For example, the original Constitution left voting qualifications to the States, though the Founders generally agreed that voters should be independent citizens with a stake in society's success. Property ownership was often required—not as a measure of worth, but as evidence of independence and productivity.

In a restored republic, qualification might include: demonstrated understanding of the Constitution and Bill of Rights (through testing), legal age and citizenship, financial independence (not receiving government assistance), and no recent conviction of rights-violating crimes. The key principle is that voters should understand what they're protecting and not have conflicts of interest in expanding government power, such as those receiving welfare.

Such qualifications do not diminish anyone's inherent rights — only their influence over others through the ballot box.

Regardless of whether a person has the right to vote or not, it would not preclude him from enjoying the freedoms and opportunities afforded by a free society, which should include the opportunity to become qualified to vote.

Chapter Fourteen
How a Republic can Remain a Free Society

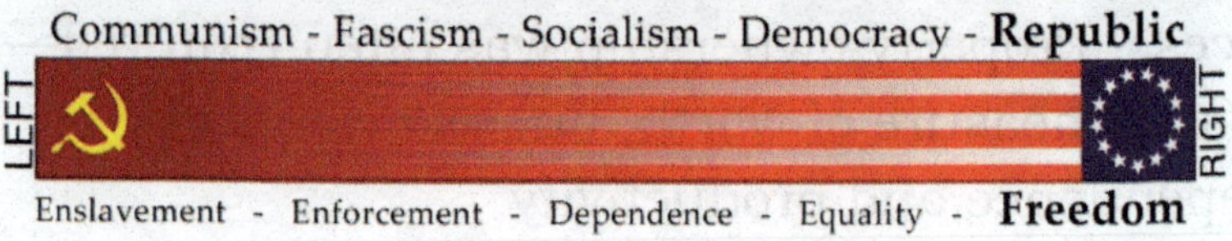

Who's Responsible?

Who ultimately is responsible for stopping the decay of freedom in America?

The government?

No. It is you. It is me.

This is Our country. It is Our government. If our government is not working right, if it is becoming oppressive, if it has been high jacked by freedom's enemies, it is your responsibility and duty to fix it. It is my responsibility and duty to fix it.

Either become active or find someone you can support. Freedom is not free. It has never been.

The Path Back

The communist list of objectives in Chapter Eight gives us a road map back toward freedom and real human rights.

The points they have attacked are the same points we must bring back into alignment with freedom.

It is as simple as that. Education, news media, justice, local government, etc.

Pick an area you have some knowledge or expertise and join with others to start winning these areas back.

Education Is the Key

The virtues of a republic are the very things which can save it or bring it down.

Education is the first vital step. It should be no surprise that our education system has been under attack and does not result in educated children.

Teachers Unions and the Federal Department of Education have been used by the far Left to bring down our culture, our freedoms and rights.

> ***"Educate and inform the whole mass of the people... They are the only sure reliance for the preservation of our liberty."***
>
> Thomas Jefferson

There are good teachers out there. They should understand what they are facing. Perhaps some will just walk away and work in private schools. Or perhaps they will take even more responsibility for taking back the education system.

Regaining control of education will be fought against, hard and long, by "teachers unions", "the Press", "liberals", oh my! It will be noisy.

These same people are solely responsible for the decline of our society's educational standards. However, the voices for freedom far outnumber those who oppress. The fight must be waged, and it must be won.

It will strike such a deep blow, the enemy will go quite mad, and probably not quietly as seen in Wisconsin in 2011-2012.

On an immediate basis, the founding documents of the Republic must be made known to and understood by as many citizens as possible.

Community discussion groups should be started all over the country by local enthusiasts with lessons on the Constitution and Bill of Rights.

These movements are already happening to some degree. If you are not part of it, join in. Your freedom depends on it.

Talk radio hosts should be encouraged to join the campaign to educate society on the founding documents. Though they do help to draw attention to the Left's activities, constant discussion of how the Left is wrong does not make the Right right. The Right is more right when it forwards its own ideas, based on the concepts of a republic.

A portion of their time would be extremely beneficial if aimed at promoting the concepts of freedom, the Constitution and the ideal scene that we should strive to achieve to build a true republic.

A grassroots campaign can be started by members of the Tea Party, whether republican, democrat or independent. They will probably take responsibility for the bulk of this effort.

These are the people who have already noticed things are not as they should be and have started to take responsibility. Their alertness and willingness to fight back can be used to forward this effort.

There are now several very good translated-to-modern-language forms of our founding documents. Books like THE PEOPLE'S GUIDE TO THE UNITED STATES CONSTITUTION provides easy to understand glossaries so it is easy to understand the documents in their original form.

Lessons created in picture form for adults and children would be helpful.

Video demonstrations of the principles of our Republic should be found or created and run on public television, which should be Public Television's first and foremost purpose.

Public Television needs to be taken back from the Left and become a tool of education, not propaganda.

Every effort to educate the populace and the next generations in our public and private schools is vital to recovering the Republic.

Private schools already lead the charge on this. Without a good education on the basics of a republic, there is nothing from which a person can compare the remaining political systems.

Artists and writers can create art which envisions the future republic based on rights and freedoms.

A full understanding of the political spectrum is vital to raise society back up toward a republic and prevent its descent into fascism.

The necessity to educate every student on the fundamentals of each and every political system on the spectrum must be understood.

This should not be just a cursory understanding, but an in-depth understanding of the philosophies, workings and downfalls of each point of the spectrum—not as propaganda, but as a look at government's role in relation to its citizens, slavery and freedom.

The covert methods used by communism to attack a free society are especially vital for people to understand so they can recognize them when they see them.

Education on the free-market system, capitalism and the covert use of capitalism to control government and societies should be included in education.

Legislative bills must be introduced into the House of Representatives to regain control over education. A key aspect of this is simply to ensure that the founding documents are presented to each class level in a format that can be understood.

We can fight this battle locally through our government system with a show of numbers and win.

If one wishes to see who the enemies of our country are, implementation of any part of this plan will certainly bring them out.

Any resurgence of the Republic will be fought bitterly. One should expect some chaos to ensue, not by the Right, but by the far Left. Concentrate on bringing order. Ignore their confusion.

Their outbursts should be ignored, while police maintain order. This plan must be brought into being quickly and urgently, if the Republic is to be salvaged.

Communism (or tyranny by any name) will not be successful if its methods are understood. It is made up of a very small percentage of the population. This group wreaks havoc on our way of life.

But they do not have to be hunted down unless they break the law. They are dangerous only when their methods are unknown. As people understand their methods, the less they are affected by them.

Thus, we can maintain freedom of speech, even for the Communist Party and yet remove the danger they present to the Republic.

THE PRESS

As for the use of the mainstream Press by the communist party, this can be remedied without reducing the freedom of the Press.

Through the educational steps above, many in the press will begin to understand how they have been used and will start to straighten themselves out.

Others will howl and scream. You will know why. More people will see their real colors and know who they are. People will stop listening.

Let them disclose their true intentions. We do not have to strip them of their rights to make them ineffective.

Capitalism and Government

Capitalism has its purpose. When used as a tool to increase economic production within the private sector, it is a worthwhile endeavor and should be supported.

The financing of government operations by private institutions, groups and individuals, such as central banks, the Federal Reserve, etc., should be strictly outlawed in a free society.

It should be made a treasonous act for those in government to secretly accept money from private sources. All such gifts or loans must be reported and made a matter of public record, if allowed at all. People in government should not be able to use their power for personal gain.

Investment by private capital into our government is an investment against freedom and is as destructive to freedom as tyranny and communism.

In fact, such investments are the only means of financing which allows communism to evolve and survive. It may be a truism that behind every fascist and communist can be found a capitalist, funding his activities.

You will find that in any war, both parties are usually heavily financed by the same or associated capitalists. These lenders expect to profit through the interest on the loans required by each government to fund the war. As a result, freedom and prosperity is reduced for all.

The book, THE NAKED CAPITALIST, reveals the names and companies who have been behind these suppressive activities. It is well worth reading. You should know those who have been working to take away your freedoms.

A parting word from the enemies of freedom:

"This struggle must be organized, according to "all the rules of the art", by people who are professionally engaged in revolutionary activity. The fact that the masses are spontaneously being drawn into the movement does not make the organization of this struggle less necessary. On the contrary, it makes it more necessary."

"A revolutionary class cannot but wish for the defeat of its government in a reactionary war."
Vladimir Lenin

Why is America different?

A free society, who is its own government, has no reason to "defeat its government". A free society can only be defeated by secretly, slowly and consistently moving its government to the left of the spectrum until that government becomes oppressive (fascist) and thus must be defeated by its own people.

Through education and alertness, a free people will not be "drawn in", but will simply spit out the hook of dependence and oppression, and continue to strive to build a nation where all people are equal under the law, where prosperity is possible for those who wish to achieve it and to set a shining example to the rest of the world's populations to rekindle their own hopes for freedom.

Shall we?

Reference

"After Socialism, Fascism combats the whole complex system of democratic ideology, and repudiates it, whether in its theoretical premises or in its practical application. Fascism denies that the majority, by the simple fact that it is a majority, can direct human society; it denies that numbers alone can govern by means of a periodical consultation, and it affirms the immutable, beneficial, and fruitful inequality of mankind, which can never be permanently leveled through the mere operation of a mechanical process such as universal suffrage.... (Paraphrased in Chapter 5, Democracy section)

NOTE ON SOURCES:

This book synthesizes information from historical documents, political writings, and publicly available sources. Key primary sources include:

- The Declaration of Independence (1776)
- The United States Constitution (1789)
- The Bill of Rights (1791)
- Works by Karl Marx, including The Communist Manifesto
- Works by Vladimir Lenin, including "What Is to Be Done?" (1902)
- Works by Joseph Stalin, including "The Press as a Collective Organizer" (1923)
- Nationalism writings on Fascism

- W. Cleon Skousen's The Naked Communist (1958)
- Congressional Record, January 10, 1963 (Communist Goals)

Statistical data regarding education, mental health, and veteran suicide rates are drawn from U.S. Department of Education reports, Department of Veterans Affairs data, and publicly available research studies current as of 2025.

Readers are encouraged to verify all claims through independent research and primary source documents.

Suggested Reading Section

THE PEOPLE'S GUIDE TO THE UNITED STATES CONSTITUTION by Dave Kluge, available on Amazon.com and Barnes & Noble

THE NAKED COMMUNIST (1958) W. Cleon Skousen, Amazon.com

THE NAKED CAPITALIST (1998) W. Cleon Skousen, Amazon.com. This book is a review and commentary on Dr. Carroll Quigley's book TRAGEDY AND HOPE, which reveals the names, intentions and scope of capitalists who back the progression of communist and finance governments around the world.

Tragedy and Hope: A History of the World in Our Time by Carroll Quigley (June 1975)

GLOSSARY

Black Market: The illegal sale and distribution of officially controlled commodities. In the United States, drugs are sold on the black market. In a communist country, food, appliances, and other goods, if not obtained through official channels, are bought and sold on the black market.

Bureaucracy: Excessive multiplication of, and concentration of power in, bureaus or administrators.

Capitulate: To stop resisting an opponent or give into an unwanted demand.

Constitution, the: The basic written set of principles and precedents of federal government in the U.S., which came into operation in 1789 and has since been modified by twenty-seven amendments.

Demagogic: Of or like a Demagogue.

Demagogue: A political leader who seeks support by appealing to popular desires and prejudices rather than by using rational argument.

Dichotomy: (die kot' o me) Division into two parts or classifications, especially when they are sharply distinguished or opposed.

Electorate: Those citizens who have earned the right and privilege to vote in elections.

Equitable: Fair and impartial.

Free Market: An economic system in which prices are determined by unrestricted competition between privately owned businesses, with minimal government interference.

Inalienable Rights: Rights that cannot be given away or taken away by their possessor. These are freedoms inherent to being human, such as life, liberty, and the pursuit of happiness.

Myriad: Countless or extremely great number of people or things.

Nazis: Members of the National Socialist German Worker's Party.

Providence: God or nature as providing protective care.

Rail: To express objection to in bitter, abusive or harsh language.

Revealed Religion: Religion based on divine revelation from God to mankind.

Self-Governance: The practice of individuals governing their own actions based on respect for the inalienable rights of others, requiring minimal external government intervention.

Social Religion: Adaption of religion that stresses social responsibility and supports the concepts of socialism. (You can find people arguing that Jesus was the "first Socialist." Such statements are made with the sole purpose of getting people to think well of Socialism and accept its doctrine.)

Tangible: Perceptible by touch; that which can be touched.

Tenet: An opinion, doctrine or principle held as being true by an organization.

Tyranny: A government in which a single ruler is vested with absolute power.

About the Author

David R. Young, a successful businessman and professional home designer. He performed as a solo singer/songwriter in his 20s on the Jersey shore. David has been interested in and has studied religious philosophy and the spiritual nature of man for the past 50 years.

A registered Independent, now Republican, who has always voted with an eye toward the Constitution, David began studying the political spectrum in August of 2011.

He soon realized there was no definitive work on the subject and set out to clarify the subject for himself. What he came to understand about the political spectrum culminated in his first published work in 2012. This is the Second Edition of his award winning work.

David lives in Clearwater, Florida with his wife and son.

You can email David at **dryoung.freedom@gmail.com**. He is interested in hearing your view of the subjects he writes about.

Made in the USA
Monee, IL
04 February 2026

43376551R00095